JUDE

JUDE

An Oral and Performance Commentary

DAVID SEAL

WIPF & STOCK · Eugene, Oregon

JUDE
An Oral and Performance Commentary

Copyright © 2021 David Seal. All rights reserved. Except for brief quotations in critical publications or reviews, no part of this book may be reproduced in any manner without prior written permission from the publisher. Write: Permissions, Wipf and Stock Publishers, 199 W. 8th Ave., Suite 3, Eugene, OR 97401.

Wipf & Stock
An Imprint of Wipf and Stock Publishers
199 W. 8th Ave., Suite 3
Eugene, OR 97401

www.wipfandstock.com

PAPERBACK ISBN: 978-1-6667-3029-6
HARDCOVER ISBN: 978-1-6667-2158-4
EBOOK ISBN: 978-1-6667-2159-1

NOVEMBER 22, 2021

Permissions

Scripture quotations marked (NRSV) are from New Revised Standard Version Bible, copyright © 1989 National Council of the Churches of Christ in the United States of America. Used by permission. All rights reserved worldwide.

Scripture quotations marked (NLT) are taken from the Holy Bible, New Living Translation, copyright ©1996, 2004, 2015 by Tyndale House Foundation. Used by permission of Tyndale House Publishers, Carol Stream, Illinois 60188. All rights reserved.

Scripture marked (NIV) is taken from the Holy Bible, NEW INTERNATIONAL VERSION®, NIV® Copyright © 1973, 1978, 1984, 2011 by Biblica, Inc.® Used by permission. All rights reserved worldwide.

Scripture quoted by permission. Quotations designated (NET) are from the NET Bible® copyright ©1996, 2019 by Biblical Studies Press, L.L.C. http://netbible.com All rights reserved.

Scripture quotations marked (ESV) are from the ESV® Bible (The Holy Bible, English Standard Version®), copyright © 2001 by Crossway, a publishing ministry of Good News Publishers. Used by permission. All rights reserved.

Scripture marked (NKJV) is taken from the New King James Version®. Copyright © 1982 by Thomas Nelson. Used by permission. All rights reserved.

Contents

Abbreviations | viii

1 INTRODUCTION | 1

2 THE ORAL AND PERFORMANCE CULTURE OF
   THE FIRST-CENTURY MEDITERRANEAN WORLD | 11

3 NEW TESTAMENT LETTERS, LECTORS,
   PERFORMANCE, AND PRESENCE | 20

4 APPROACH OF THIS COMMENTARY | 28

5 COMMENTARY ON JUDE | 30

Bibliography | 95

Abbreviations

GENERAL

BCE	Before the Common Era
BDAG	Bauer, W., F. W. Danker, W. F. Arndt, and F. W. Gingrich
BDB	Brown, Francis, Samuel Rolles Driver, and Charles Augustus Briggs
ca.	circa
CE	Common Era
cf.	confer
ch.	chapter
chs.	chapters
ed(s).	editor(s)
e.g.	for example
esp.	especially
ESV	English Standard Version
et al.	et alia
LXX	Septuagint
n.d.	no date
NET	New English Translation
NIV	New International Version
NKJV	New King James Version
NLT	New Living Translation
n.p.	no pages

Abbreviations

NRSV	New Revised Standard Version
trans.	translated
v.	verse
vv.	verses
Vol.	volume

HEBREW BIBLE/OLD TESTAMENT

Gen	Genesis
Exod	Exodus
Lev	Leviticus
Num	Numbers
Deut	Deuteronomy
Josh	Joshua
Judg	Judges
Ruth	Ruth
1–2 Sam	1–2 Samuel
1–2 Kgs	1–2 Kings
1–2 Chr	1–2 Chronicles
Ezra	Ezra
Neh	Nehemiah
Esth	Esther
Job	Job
Ps/Pss	Psalms
Prov	Proverbs
Eccl	Ecclesiastes
Song	Song of Songs (Song of Solomon)
Isa	Isaiah
Jer	Jeremiah
Lam	Lamentations
Ezek	Ezekiel
Dan	Daniel
Hos	Hosea
Joel	Joel
Amos	Amos
Obad	Obadiah

ABBREVIATIONS

Jonah	Jonah
Mic	Micah
Nah	Nahum
Hab	Habakkuk
Zeph	Zephaniah
Hag	Haggai
Zech	Zechariah
Mal	Malachi

NEW TESTAMENT

Matt	Matthew
Mark	Mark
Luke	Luke
John	John
Acts	Acts
Rom	Romans
1–2 Cor	1–2 Corinthians
Gal	Galatians
Eph	Ephesians
Phil	Philippians
Col	Colossians
1–2 Thess	1–2 Thessalonians
1–2 Tim	1–2 Timothy
Titus	Titus
Phlm	Philemon
Heb	Hebrews
Jas	James
1–2 Pet	1–2 Peter
1–2–3 John	1–2–3 John
Jude	Jude
Rev	Revelation

1

Introduction

JUDE IS A SHORT LETTER making it easy to read entirely in one sitting. Yet the letter is rarely read, and it is not a popular text for teaching and preaching. One reason for its neglect is that Jude writes to a unique audience capable of understanding his Old Testament references as well as his references to books outside the Bible such as 1 *Enoch* and *The Assumption of Moses*. These books, especially 1 *Enoch*, circulated widely among the believers of the first century. References from 1 *Enoch*, *The Assumption of Moses*, and perhaps even some from Scripture are less familiar to the contemporary reader. To better understand the message of Jude, these references, and allusions from outside the Bible require some explanation.

Jude uses various examples from non-biblical and biblical sources to warn about a group of itinerant teachers bearing a message that Jude considers incompatible with the apostolic gospel. The teaching and practice of these people puts them into a class of individuals who, according to Scripture, incur God's wrath and judgment. Thus, they constitute a severe danger, which Jude's readers must resist. Jude stresses that there is guaranteed judgment on those who live outside the normalized instruction and teach others to do the same.

The importance of a lifestyle that adheres with biblical teaching is just as crucial today as it was in the early church. Contemporary culture is becoming more and more indifferent to the question of truth. Jude is a book about the dangers of this issue transpiring. In addition to offering encouragement to the recipients, Jude warns Christians that they must always remain alert, guarding against any compromise to biblical teaching in their lives and the church.

Following a discussion of the letter's author, date, recipients, occasion, genre, structure, relationship to 2 Peter, and canonization, there will be an overview of the oral and performative nature of the first century Mediterranean world. Jude was situated in this oral context, and it decisively shaped the form and delivery of the epistle while also enhancing its content. One cannot separate the content of a message from how a message comes to expression. This commentary aims to show the relationship between expression and content, demonstrating that there is not only value in *what* Jude says but in *how* he says it.

AUTHOR

Like many of the Apostle Paul's letters in the New Testament (e.g., Gal 1:1; Phil 1:1; 1 Thess 1:1; 2 Thess 1:1), the author of the book of Jude identifies himself in the letter opening (v. 1). He states that he is Jude (*Ioúdas* [Judas] in Greek),[1] a servant of Jesus Christ and brother of James. Several people in the New Testament and certain extra-biblical sources are mentioned with some form of the name "Jude/Judas."[2] The two most accepted views of authorship

---

1. Traditionally the name is translated "Jude" in English versions to distinguish from the Judas that betrayed Jesus (New English Translation Bible [NET], Full Notes Edition, 2351).

2. Judas the brother of James and Joseph and Simon (Matt 13:55; Mark 6:3); Judas the son of James (Luke 6:16; Acts 1:13), who may be the same person as "Judas, not Iscariot" in John 14:22; Judas Iscariot (e.g., Matt 10:4; 26:14, 25); Judas the Galilean, a revolutionary (Acts 5:37); Judas of Damascus (Acts 9:11); Judas Barsabbas (Acts 15:22, 27, 32). Several noncanonical works mention Judas but are questionable because of their limited geographical

Introduction

are either Jude, the half-brother of Jesus (and brother of James), or someone claiming to be Jude who wrote the letter under a pseudonym. Those who take the author to be Jude the brother of Jesus base this on the author's claim to be "the brother of James," who is then assumed to be James the Just, the Lord's brother (Matt 13:55; Mark 6:3).[3]

The Greek vocabulary and literary style are considered by some to be too good to have been written by a Galilean artisan's (Joseph the carpenter) son,[4] supporting that the letter was possibly written under a pseudonym. However, a trusted and trained scribe could have assisted Jude as a secretary, an editor, or a coauthor. Paul's practice of letter writing often involved dictating his thoughts to a secretary (Rom 16:22).

Lacking any firm evidence, it is impossible to decisively prove any of the options for authorship. Rather than considering the known individuals that are named Jude in the New Testament or extra-biblical sources, it is more beneficial to consider the identity of the author based on his self-portrayal within the letter. We will discuss the author's self-portrayal later in the discussion of verse 1.[5] Regardless of the identity of the writer, the authority of the letter rests upon the designation "servant of Jesus Christ."

DATE

Conclusions about authorship also affect decisions about when Jude was composed. The letter may have been written as early as the first letters of Paul (ca. 50s CE) or have been composed from a period as late as 80–85 CE, if Jude was Jesus's younger brother,

---

distribution, biased theological agenda, and they lack support from any canonical source (Eusebius, *Ecclesiastical History* 1.13; 6.13; 6.14; the *Gospel of Thomas* Prologue; Noted by Neyrey [2 *Peter, Jude*, 30]).

3. James is referred to as "the Just" because of his piety and reverence for the law (Eusebius, *Ecclesiastical History* 2.1.1–5). As noted by Viktor Roudkovski ("James, Brother of Jesus," n.p.).

4. See Steven J. Kraftchick for an example of this view (*Jude & 2 Peter*, 21).

5. For an extensive discussion of authorship see Bateman, *Jude*, 11–19.

since the latter period is the approximate outer limit for Jude's life span. If, however, Jude is considered pseudepigraphic, then the letter was likely written during the postapostolic age (ca. 80s–160s CE).

The relationship of 2 Peter to Jude also affects the dating of the book. Many similarities exist between these two works, suggesting some level of borrowing of one text by the other or that both authors used a common source.[6] Assuming the accuracy of the tradition that Peter was martyred under Nero, if Simon Peter bar Jonah wrote 2 Peter, it was probably written before 68 CE, the date of the Roman emperor Nero's death.[7] That would mean Jude was composed around 60 CE at the latest, given that Peter would have to get it and read it before he could use it. However, if 2 Peter is a posthumous document, then the dates of 2 Peter and of Jude could easily be a couple of decades later.[8] Given the correlation between the author of Jude, the text's relationship to 2 Peter and the book's date of composition, it is difficult to take a firm position about when Jude was written.

RECIPIENTS

Jude does not address a specific group of Christians, nor does he disclose their location. Herbert Bateman contends that if Jude, the brother of James wrote the letter, he was likely writing to Jewish Christians in Judaea.[9] On the other hand, if Jude is pseudepigraphic, then the letter's destination was likely to Gentile Christians living in Asia Minor, Syrian Antioch, or Alexandrian Egypt.[10]

Given that Jude does not designate the location of his recipients has led some scholars to infer that the epistle was meant to be a "general" one, with broad application to be read by numerous

---

6. See the discussion on the relationship of 2 Peter to Jude later in the Introduction.
7. Davids, *Letters of 2 Peter and Jude*, 12.
8. Davids, *Letters of 2 Peter and Jude*, 12.
9. Bateman, *Jude*, 27.
10. Bateman, *Jude*, 27.

churches. This is unlikely in view of its brevity and the distinctive nature of the errors Jude mentions. Further, the letter contains hints that the author had a specific emergency affecting a particular community or communities in mind.[11]

For more specifics about the addressees, we must examine the information in the letter to determine what we can about the recipients. Jude's readers were either Gentile or Jewish Christians or a combination of both. One factor that supports an entirely Jewish audience is the author's reference to numerous events and people from Hebrew Scriptures[12] (Jude 5, 6, 7, 9, 11) and traditions preserved in the Second Temple texts of 1 *Enoch* and the *Assumption of Moses*. A Jewish audience would have been familiar with these references.[13] It is unlikely that Jude would have quoted from or alluded to sources that were not part of his audience's verbal repertoire and ones that were not held in high esteem.[14] However, it is possible a Gentile audience might be acquainted with Hebrew Scriptures. For example, Luke, a Gentile, was knowledgeable in the Hebrew Scriptures. Gentile God-fearers in Acts appear competent in the Jewish Scriptures (Acts 13:26; 16:14). The epistle of 1 Peter contains numerous Old Testament quotations, but was sent to Gentile churches in Pontus, Galatia, Cappadocia, Asia, and Bithynia.[15]

OCCASION

The book of Jude is mostly a plethora of condemning statements against certain outsiders (v. 4) who have infiltrated the church and are considered by the author to be detrimental to the sacredness

---

11. Kelly, *Epistles of Peter and of Jude*, 242–43.

12. "Hebrew Bible" and "Hebrew Scriptures" are often used to refer to the Hebrew books of the Old Testament. "Old Testament" is a Christian label for the Jewish Scriptures that preceded the New Testament.

13. Copies of *Enoch* have been found in multiple caves at Qumran. See Nickelsburg, 1 *Enoch* 1, 12.

14. Joubert, "Language, Ideology," 340.

15. Bateman, *Jude*, 28.

and health of the Christian community. While they are depicted as outsiders (v. 4), the dangerous individuals seem to be present at the church's sacred supper ("the Lord's Supper," v. 12), and were around long enough to cause divisions in the congregation (v. 19). Even though they claim to be followers of Christ (v. 4) the overarching sin of the intruders is their rejection of all moral authority, whether that of the law of Moses (vv. 8–10) or that of Christ himself (vv. 4, 8). This behavior is often called antinomianism, which simply means "antilawism," having no regard for the law. [16]

While these individuals can be clearly seen as adversaries of Christianity, and thus, opponents of Jude, the author uses a variety of labels and infers much about their nature. Labels that Jude uses include intruders (v. 4), ungodly (vv. 4, 15), dreamers (v. 8), false teachers (v. 11), sinners (v. 15), scoffers (v. 18), worldly, void of God's Spirit, and divisive (v. 19). Further, in a derisive manner, Jude repeatedly identifies the adversaries by the pronoun "these" (e.g., v. 14). This type of presentation portrays them in the most undesirable manner possible, personifying them as faceless individuals.[17] Some scholars have identified these outsiders as Gnostic.[18] However, there is no evidence of the characteristic teaching of the Gnostics, such as the denigration of physical matter or of Gnostic creation myths involving an inferior deity's fashioning of the physical world.[19] Recently Herbert Bateman, taking into consideration Judaea's sociopolitical events leading up to the Judaean revolt against Rome (66 CE), which was pursued intensely by Jewish Zealots, argues that Jude's attack was aimed at these Zealots and all those who were coerced to join them.[20]

In view of Jude's use of excessive, amplified, and villainous rhetorical language to describe his opponents, the connection between these descriptions and their real-life counterparts is

---

16. Sproul, *How Should I Live in This World?* 40.
17. Joubert, "Persuasion in the Letter of Jude," 83.
18. E.g., Kelly, *Epistles of Peter and of Jude*, 231.
19. Painter and deSilva, *James and Jude*, 183.
20. See Bateman's full argument in *Jude*, 50–81.

Introduction

probably not a one-to-one relationship.²¹ As noted by William Brosend, "Twenty-five charges in twenty-five verses is a high rate of accusation."²² Since the language is aimed at persuading the audience not to be influenced by the adversaries, an element of distortion or excess should be expected. However, for these accusations against the opponents to have any persuasiveness, there must be some overlap between rhetoric and reality.²³

Given Christian ethical standards, it might be thought that the *ēthos*²⁴ of a writer would be undermined if he were perceived as untrustworthy. However, in antiquity, an excessive and stereotypical portrayal of one's opponents was known and accepted by both speaker and listeners.²⁵ This use of excess rhetoric in Jude can be compared to modern day political speeches.

GENRE AND STRUCTURE

Jude has only the outward appearance of a letter containing a standard greeting, a body, and a formulaic conclusion. While the body opening employs a standard writing formula (v. 2), the concluding doxology (vv. 24–25) resembles that of a homiletic or liturgical form rather than a typical letter closing. The presence of the doxology suggests that Jude intended for his letter to be read as the homily for the congregation assembled for worship. As Richard Bauckham said, it is appropriate then to refer to Jude as an "epistolary sermon," where its content could have been delivered as a homily to the recipients whom Jude could not visit in person.²⁶ Duane Watson argues that early Christian letters were substitutes

---

21. Du Toit, "Vilification as a Pragmatic Device," 54–55.
22. Brosend, "Letter of Jude," 301.
23. Donelson, *I and II Peter, and Jude*, 196.
24. In the ancient world, the strength of an argument relied on the moral authority of the author (*ēthos*).
25. Thurén, "Hey Jude!" 458.
26. Bauckham, 2 *Peter, Jude*, 3.

for giving an oral address in person. They were designed as speeches in letter form.[27]

There are certain clues in Jude, indicating it was situated in and written for a primarily oral culture to be read out loud. Jude divulges its oral dimension by using techniques such as alliteration (cf. vv. 3, 4) and homoeoteleuton (v. 8), rhetorical devices that are best experienced when a text is spoken out loud. His use of triplets throughout the letter serve to capture and maintain the listeners' attention. Finally, the doxology at the end is formulated in such a way that it could be spoken antiphonally, inviting the audience's participation in the doxology. Details about these and other oral techniques will be explicated in detail later in the commentary.

Though it does not contain all the characteristics of a typical first-century letter, Jude can be divided into three "epistolary" parts. The letter opens with a greeting, identifying the author and audience. As noted, the author characterizes himself by two designations: "a servant of Jesus Christ" and "a brother of James" (v. 1).[28] The recipients of this letter are addressed in such a way that stresses three dimensions of God's activity (v. 1). The recipients of the letter are "called," "beloved in God the Father," and "kept safe for Jesus Christ." Jude concludes his introduction with "May mercy, peace, and love be yours in abundance" (v. 2).

The body of the letter has two parts. Verses 3–19 identify the opponents, warns of their danger, their behavior, and their punishment. To describe these opponents and their certain punishment, Jude uses illustrations and examples from biblical history (vv. 5–7; 11), nature (vv. 12–13), and teachings found outside the Bible (vv. 9; 14–15).[29] The opponents rejected all moral authority and believed they were free to use their own standards to determine what behavior was correct for them.

The second section of the letter's body (vv. 20–23) offers advice on how the church is to respond to those that have been

27. Watson, "Epistolary Rhetoric of 1 Peter, 2 Peter, and Jude," 48.

28. All biblical quotations are from the NRSV unless otherwise noted.

29. The extra-biblical sources are mainly 1 *Enoch, Assumption of Moses, Testament of Reuben,* and *Jubilees.*

influenced by the false teachers. Jude calls on the church to grow in their understanding of their faith (v. 20), be assured of their salvation (v. 21) and help those who have fallen prey to the practices and teaching of the opponents (vv. 22–23).

Jude concludes with a doxology (24–25). It divides into four parts: first, the person praised, "the only God our Savior"; second, the word of praise, "glory, majesty, power, and authority"; third, the indication of time is given, "before all time and now and forever"; and finally, a closing, "Amen," representing the response with which the hearers affirm the content of the prayer.

JUDE'S RELATIONSHIP TO 2 PETER

There is a clear literary relationship between Jude and 2 Peter, leading scholars to conclude that based on the extensive similarities it appears one author made use of the other or they both used a common source. The similarities are largely between Jude 4–13, 16–18, and 2 Pet 2:1–18; 3:1–3. The similarities between the two compositions could be explained as the result of both authors using a common source. However, the source appears to be almost parallel to Jude, "which raises the question of why Jude would have used a source to which he added nothing besides an epistolary framework (vv. 1–3, 24–25) and a brief exhortation (vv. 20–23)?"[30]

Similarities could also be explained by one author borrowing from the other. One important reason for preferring 2 Peter's use of Jude to the opposite hypothesis is that 2 Peter, the longer letter, used the shorter Jude and expanded on it rather than vice versa. However, this reasoning is not convincing to all.[31] It is certainly possible that Jude may have wanted to extract certain ideas from 2 Peter that were relevant to his situation. In the end, Michael Green is probably correct to say that because many of the arguments can

---

30. Hultin, "Literary Relationships," 37. For a balanced presentation of the relationship between 2 Peter and Jude see Green, *2 Peter and Jude*, 68–74.

31. E.g., Moo, *2 Peter, Jude*, 18.

support a borrowing in either direction it is likely we shall never reach a conclusion about the relationship between the two texts.[32]

CANONIZATION

If 2 Peter utilized Jude and if Peter wrote 2 Peter (both positions are disputed), then 2 Peter is the oldest witness to Jude, and its canonicity, in principle, is settled at a very early date.[33] In the writings of the early church fathers, several allusions to Jude have been identified.[34] By the end of the second century Jude was widely accepted as Scripture by Tertullian in North Africa, Clement and Origen in Alexandria, and the Muratorian Canon in Italy.[35]

After this general acceptance, later doubts about the book arose. The church historian Eusebius lists Jude among the disputed writings contested by the church (*Ecclesiastical History* 1.13; 6.13; 6.14). Jude's major problem was its references to the non-canonical books 1 *Enoch* and the *Assumption of Moses*.[36] These books, especially 1 *Enoch*, circulated widely among the believers of the first century and were theologically influential—likely one reason Jude used them. Despite being disputed, Athanasius included Jude in his famous canon of 367 and hereafter its position was generally secure.[37]

---

32. Green, *2 Peter and Jude*, 71.

33. Blum, "Jude," n.p.

34. Cf. Bigg, *Critical and Exegetical Commentary*, 305–10.

35. Bauckham, *2 Peter, Jude*, 17. The Muratorian Canon is a fragment that identifies and briefly describes the various writings that the author regarded as authoritative. It contains one of the oldest canonical lists of the New Testament from early Christianity (Laird, "Muratorian Fragment," n.p.).

36. It is not entirely unusual for authors of Scripture to reference other writings outside the Bible. Other biblical books quote or reference non-canonical sources (e.g., Josh 10:13; Acts 17:28; 1 Cor 15:33; 2 Tim 3:8; Titus 1:12). It is noteworthy that Jude does not call the non-canonical sources "Scripture." A high view of inspiration does not preclude the inspired author's right to quote from non-biblical sources (Wheaton, "Jude," 1274).

37. Kelly, *Epistles of Peter and of Jude*, 223–24. Athanasius of Alexandria (ca. 293–373 CE) was a theologian, the bishop of Alexandria, and an influential leader in Egypt during the fourth century. He is notable for being the first to use the word "canon" to refer to the New Testament (as we currently know it) in his festal letter of 367 CE (Wierenga, "Church Fathers," n.p.).

2

The Oral and Performance Culture of the First-Century Mediterranean World

ORAL CULTURES AND THEIR CHARACTERISTICS

BECAUSE JUDE WAS WRITTEN and then later recited aloud before an audience, it is important to provide some details about the oral nature of the first century Mediterranean world. Most public communication in the first-century Mediterranean culture was oral. Examples of oral communication would have included speeches in the assembly, in the council, and in the law courts, public announcements, lectures, invitations to banquets, acclamations, gossip, slander, oaths, hymns, curses, prayers, confessions, and advertisements in the market, just to mention a few.[1] Consequently, most ancient texts were composed with their aural[2] and oral potential in mind, and they were meant to be delivered orally when they arrived at their destinations.[3]

---

1. Chaniotis, "Listening to Stones," 302, 307.
2. The term "aural" means of or relating to the ear or to the sense of hearing.
3. Witherington III, *What's in the Word*, 35.

The first-century world was a blend of an oral and a scribal culture. It was a world familiar with writing, but still significantly, even predominately, oral. While texts and literate individuals were present in the first century Mediterranean world, most people appreciated written compositions because they heard the work's message and content by word of mouth. Oral societies have either no writing or so little experience with writing that their pre-literate expressive and intellectual habits remain mostly unchanged.[4]

Reading out loud in an oral culture was an effective way to communicate to large groups of people. Roman emperors and other officials used heralds to read official decrees aloud to subjects living in the outlying provinces of the empire.[5] Reading aloud the Jewish sacred books was a common practice in the synagogues of the first century (Philo, *That Every Good Person Is Free*, 81–82; Luke 4:16–21; Acts 13:15; 15:21).

Oral cultures tend to have certain factors that contribute to the continued preference for the spoken word over the written word. Some of the main factors include: the cumbersome nature of scrolls and bound papyrus sheets (codex); low literacy rates; the preference for hearing texts rather than reading them; and the high cost and limited availability of writing materials.

Scrolls could be difficult to unroll and re-roll without dropping them. The first century author Pliny the Younger recounts an occasion when an individual dropped a scroll because of its extreme weight.[6] Moreover, in the process of bending down to pick it up, he fractured his hip. While his alleged age of eighty-three years and frail hands may have been a factor in the incident, heavy scrolls were likely to have been the norm. Further, it is likely that not everyone had this type of experience when handling a scroll, but it does suggest scrolls were cumbersome. Around the second century CE, the codex began to replace the scroll as the dominant writing format.[7] Codices could be more robust and portable as

---

4. Hibbitts, "'Coming to Our Senses," 882.
5. See for example Cassius Dio, *Roman History* 55.34.2, 3 and 56.25.5, 6.
6. Pliny the Younger, *Epistulae* 2.1.5.
7. Vearncombe, "Codex," 52.

Oral and Performance Culture

they were bound in the center of a collection of sheets (of papyrus or parchment) and sometimes had leather covers.

A culture's low level of literacy also contributed to the preference for the spoken word over the written. Some merchants of long-distance trade probably had a limited aptitude for reading and writing for conducting their trade, or they hired literate employees to carry out these functions. In the first century Mediterranean world, one could be educated without knowing how to read or write.

Finally, the cost of producing literature made the transition from an oral to a written culture more restrained. During the mid-first century CE, one sheet of papyrus cost two obols, about one third of the average daily wage for an Egyptian worker.[8] While the wealthier population could afford papyrus for writing, for the majority, books and writing materials were considered a luxury.[9]

In addition to factors that can prohibit the transition from oral to more written modes of communication, oral cultures tend to have certain characteristics that distinguish them from non-oral cultures. First, in oral cultures, people are more skilled at remembering what they hear. People's memories serve as the storehouse of information rather than books.[10] Teachers in the rabbinical schools lectured from memory.[11] The first century writer Seneca the Elder boasted that he could repeat two thousand names in the order they were given to him, and he could recite from memory numerous lines of poetry.[12] In oral cultures, memory was trained more vigorously than it is today. Memory aids were often built into a written text. For example, in the Hebrew culture, literature used

---

8. Harris, *Ancient Literacy*, 195. For a view that papyrus was not expensive see Skeat, "Was Papyrus Regarded as 'Cheap' or 'Expensive,'" 74–93.

9. Blumell, "Message and the Medium," 28.

10. Lee and Scott, *Sound Mapping*, 92.

11. The Gemara and Mishnah make up the rabbinic Jewish text called the Talmud. In Aramaic, Gemara means acquired learning. That meaning reflects the teaching method of the rabbis, who passed on the Gemara by committing it to memory rather than writing it down ("Gemara," in Elwell and Beitzel, *Baker Encyclopedia of the Bible*, 27).

12. *Controversiae* 1, 2, Preface (Winsbury, *Roman Book*, 121).

in worship, such as Psalm 119, utilized an acrostic, where the first letter of each line of successive stanzas were successive letters in the Hebrew alphabet. This assisted the faithful in memorization of large amounts of material and allowed them to participate more fully in public worship.

Secondly, in addition to highly developed memory skills, oral societies experience literature collectively. When literature is read privately, readers must make their own interpretation of the words on the page. By contrast, when literature is performed by a lector,[13] the recipient is guided in their interpretation by the person reciting the text in front of them. The listener is directed in the interpretation of the text as they experience the reader's facial expressions, voice inflection, posture, and body language. This intimacy between reader and the audience can also allow listeners who did not know the sender to become acquainted with them and feel included more fully in the community.

THE PERFORMATIVE NATURE OF ORAL LITERATURE

Oral cultures can also be called performance cultures in the sense that speakers from these environments have fluent communication skills related to delivery.[14] To communicate more effectively, performers can employ several types of techniques simultaneously by using their voice, facial expressions, and gestures. Ancient recitations before an audience were at times dramatic, engaging, spirited, and emotional.[15] So, rather than simply referring to oral events as readings or recitations, we can call them performances.

---

13. A lector (*anagnōstēs*) is a trained reader who performs public readings from a manuscript. We will discuss their function more fully later in the chapter (cf. 1 Esdras 8:8, 9, 19; 9:39, 42, 49 LXX).

14. Aristotle, *Rhetoric* 3.12.1–3; Cicero, *De oratore* 3.52–55; Quintilian, *Institutio oratoria* 11.3.2–6; *Rhetorica ad Herennium* 3.11.19.

15. Cf. Isocrates, *Philippus* 5.25–27; Cicero, *De oratore* 1.25–27; Suetonius, *De poetis, Vitellius* 25; Ezek 24; Jer 19.

ORAL AND PERFORMANCE CULTURE

Oral performance literature has certain features aimed at enhancing an audience's experience of the spoken text. First, the literature contains narrative and rhetorical devices to underscore important themes and arouse listener's emotions.[16] Unlike readers, who can refer backward and forward in the text, listening audiences do not have the luxury or ability to reread sections of a text to determine meaning semantically. Thus, ancient authors of oral literature relied upon oral cues such as alliteration, homoeoteleuton (a sound technique that reiterates a series of words or phrases with similar endings), and onomatopoeia.[17] These devices serve to draw attention to a thought, word, or idea that the writer felt was important.

The effect of the rhetorical/oratorical devices previously considered depends on how they are delivered, which includes both the voice and the body of the speaker. Aristotle discussed how the voice should be adapted to express different emotions (*Rhetoric* 3.1, see also Plato, *Ion* 535b-e6).[18] Cicero remarked that one speaker's use of pauses, exclamations, and a deep voice was so effective that they made up for certain other speaking skills he lacked (Cicero, *Brutus*, 234-35). He also stated that the orator needs the vocal power of tragic performers (*De oratore* 1.128). Given the attention devoted to one's speaking voice it is no surprise that the comic actor Hermon missed his entrance at a competition because he was preparing his voice outside.[19]

In addition, speakers can also impersonate. Impersonation was a tool of ancient orators and lawyers in court as they delivered their speeches and acted as a defense or prosecuting attorney.[20] Quintilian, a Roman orator, named an orphan, a shipwrecked man, and a person in grave peril as some of the personas that his

---

16. Cf. Dionysius of Halicarnassus, *De Demosthene* 40.

17. For a variety of other ancient rhetorical devices see Anderson Jr., *Glossary of Greek Rhetorical Terms*.

18. As noted by Murray, "Poetic Inspiration," 163.

19. Arnott, *Public and Performance*, 81.

20. Demetrius, *De elocutione* 265-266; cf. Cicero, *Pro Caelio* 33-38; Quintilian, *Institutio oratoria* 11.1.39.

students may have to mimic when speaking in the law courts.[21] For Quintilian, impersonation was an important component of persuasive speech. The reader performing a biblical passage could impersonate people through various means including, but not limited to, consideration of the person's age, sex, and social status.

Emotion is another vocal feature that can be expressed by a speaker's voice. Aristotle discussed how the voice should be adapted to express different emotions.[22] In his rhetorical handbook for training speakers, Quintilian stated that the orator should aspire to achieve the actor's skill at exhibiting the feelings of his character. He frequently observed comic and tragic actors so engrossed in their roles that after having performed a melancholy scene and taken off their masks, they were still in tears.[23] Instances where emotions are directly mentioned or implied in the text offer the speaker an opportunity to communicate these feelings to a listening audience.

In addition, it would have been important for a speaker to be able to adapt his voice to bring out the character and meaning of the passage. Aristotle discussed how the voice should be adapted to express different emotions (*Rhetoric* 3.1). When Socrates asked Ion if he was aware that when he exhibits emotions in his performances that he generates the same feelings in his spectators, Ion replied that he was mindful of this influence he had on his audience (Plato, *Ion* 535b–e6).[24] To move an audience, the orator must genuinely feel the emotions he wishes to arouse in them (Cicero, *De Oratore* 2.189–96). The ability to move an audience is an essential part of the orator's art.

Along with the voice, the body can articulate a variety of emotions. Body language can also help to communicate other verbal messages. The body, by its "distinguishing characteristics, gender, age, motions, and positions, sends and oozes thousands

21. *Institutio oratoria* 6.2.36.
22. *Rhetoric* 3.1.
23. *Institutio oratoria* 6.2.35. Cicero also says he has often seen an actor's eyes blazing under his mask after speaking solemn lines (*De oratore* 2.193).
24. As noted by Murray, "Poetic Inspiration," 163.

Oral and Performance Culture

of messages at every moment."[25] Bodily appearance and movements accompany, reinforce, contradict, and even replace words and actions.[26] Ancient orators used gestures to express a variety of emotions.[27] In oral and written literature an author can describe various motions, indicating specific gestures to the performer. On occasion, the text will imply a mood or emotion that can be embodied. For example, there might be times when it is appropriate to bend forward slightly and stoop the shoulders to convey despair—the mood expressed in a lament passage.

The hands and arms were used by orators to display emotions and to accompany and support them in their verbal communication (Quintilian, *Institutio oratoria* 11.3.85–87).[28] Hands were used to demonstrate excitement, restrain, approval, admiration, shame, joy, sadness, doubt, confession, horror, fear, and remorse. They were also used to demand, promise, summon, dismiss, threaten, beg, inquire, deny, convey size, quantity, number, and time.

Quintilian stated that one should not only use the voice, but the whole carriage of the body for the effective delivery of a speech (*Institutio oratoria* 11.3.3). Pliny remarked that when a person read while he was seated, and while he held a scroll, then the two main aids to effective delivery and pronunciation were hindered, the eyes and the hands (*Epistulae* 2.19.4). How much dramatic movement did ancient speakers utilize in their performances? Ancient images of orators provide some insight. Richard Ward and David Trobisch describe an ancient painting on the wall of a Roman villa in Pompeii, Naples, depicting a typical oral performance.

> A robed figure is standing, speaking and clasping a scroll in the left hand. The performer's right hand is lowered, loose and at rest; an extended forefinger points to the floor of the stage. The artist has draped a toga across the left arm. The performer's face, unmasked, is a thoughtful

25. Lateiner, *Sardonic Smile*, 3.
26. Lateiner, *Sardonic Smile*, 3.
27. *Rhetorica ad Herennium* 3.13–14.
28. For visual examples of ancient gestures see Shiell, *Reading Acts*, and Aldrete, *Gestures and Acclamations*.

countenance, revealing that the piece being presented is no comic diversion; its subject is serious.[29]

From the image, it is apparent that the right hand remained free for gestures. Orators used gestures to communicate kindness, grief, emphasis, laughter, and pity to name a few (*Rhetorica ad Herennium* 3.13–14). The picture also reveals that facial expressions can convey emotions that correspond with the text being recited. Gestures can lend support to the words spoken to render them more meaningful and emotional. While the gestures described in the ancient rhetorical handbooks were used by orators, many of them were widespread in Roman society, even among the poor.[30] Because of the constant exposure to orators, the public would have likely been well-equipped in interpreting the gestures and responding to them.

In addition to the hands, the face also played an important role in good public communication (Cicero, *De oratore* 3.223). Quintilian notes that the greatest influence the speaker has is a glance. The eyes can show threats, flattery, sorrow, joy, pride, or submission (*Institutio oratoria* 11.3.75–76). The same can be said for the gaze (Cicero, *De oratore* 2.223).[31]

AUDIENCE RESPONSE AND PARTICIPATION

Ancient performances involved a performer and an audience occupying the same space at the same time. This afforded an opportunity for spectators to respond to and participate in a presentation.[32] People were familiar with being part of a crowd, listening to a speaker and being able to react, participate and articulate their approval or disapproval of what was being communicated.

---

29. Ward and Trobisch, *Bringing the Word to Life*, 3.
30. Aldrete, *Gestures and Acclamations*, 50.
31. Shiell, *Delivering from Memory*, 13.
32. For examples of audience participation and response see Pliny, *Letters* 6.17.1–3, and Cicero, *Epistulae ad Atticum* 2.19.2–3.

Oral and Performance Culture

We carry around in our heads a variety of previously heard, written, and vocal expressions. Authors rely on this storage phenomenon when composing new material because it can make their words more intelligible, and it can serve as a method for engaging listeners. Robert Alter claims, "No one writes a poem or a story without some awareness of other poems or stories to emulate, pay homage to, vie with, criticize, or parody."[33] This was also true of the authors of the Bible. When biblical texts allude to other Scripture, they evoke other settings in unexpected ways.

There are inevitable limitations and a fair amount of speculation in attempting to determine the way a biblical passage was originally delivered. The original performances are lost, but with careful attention to the remnants of features that are typically associated with orally composed works and with some imagination, we can speculate on the way performances were potentially carried out.

---

33. Alter, *World of Biblical Literature*, 110.

3

New Testament Letters, Lectors, Performance, and Presence

NEW TESTAMENT LETTERS

CHRISTIANS BEGAN SENDING AND RECEIVING apostolic letters as early as the middle of the first century (1 Thess 5:27) at their gatherings in homes, probably on the first day of the week (cf. Acts 20:7).[1] Like much of the literature in the first-century Mediterranean world, the letters written to the churches by Paul and others were read aloud to the assembly (Acts 15:22–35; Col 4:16; 1 Thess 5:27; 1 Tim 4:13; Rev 1:3; Shepherd of Hermas, *Vision* 2.4.3; Justin, *First Apology* 67.3). Ephesians 3:4 indicates that the reading of letters had become a common practice in the church.[2] Early

---

1. First Thessalonians was likely written between 49 and 52 CE, shortly after the establishment of the Thessalonian church. This can be surmised from Paul's mention of Timothy rejoining him at Corinth from Thessalonica (1 Thess 3:1–6; cf. Acts 17:13–15; 18:1, 5).

2. Scholars date Ephesians between 60 and 90 CE depending on if they affirm or deny Pauline authorship. A later date is usually offered by those denying Pauline authorship (e.g., Lincoln, *Ephesians*, lxxii).

Letters, Lectors, Performance, and Presence

Christians read literature aloud at meals (e.g., Acts 2; Acts 4).[3] The epistle of Jude was likely recited aloud to its recipients.

Like today, a letter in the ancient Mediterranean world was a written message employed because of the spatial separation of the correspondents. The letter acted as a substitute for face-to-face communication (cf. Cicero, *Epistulae ad Atticum* 8.14.1; 12.53; Seneca, *Epistulae morales* 75.1), which would presumably have taken place if the author and recipients were physically present with each other.

Composing a letter in the ancient world not only involved time and energy, but it was also financially costly. The price of a papyrus roll in Egypt during the mid-first century CE was typically four drachmae; the price of a single sheet was two obols (a third of a drachma).[4] The price would have been higher the further one lived from Egypt. The largest papyrus sheets upon which letters were normally written could hold only about two hundred and fifty words. Jude contains about four hundred and fifty-eight words.

In the ancient world the production of a manuscript even as short as a personal letter was not only costly to purchase supplies but also was a highly technical one. The duties of a scribe required specialized training. Mainly the skill to follow dictation quickly and accurately.[5] The price of a well-produced manuscript was expensive. According to a letter written during the reign of Claudius (mid-first century CE) it cost two drachmae to have a short personal letter copied on papyrus.[6] The price to compose the letter to the Ephesians is estimated to have cost seven hundred and seventy in today's dollars to cover the price of supplies and to pay a secretary to write two copies.[7] Jude is one sixth the size of

---

3. Shiell, *Delivery from Memory*, 40.
4. Reece, *Paul's Large Letters*, 15.
5. Reece, *Paul's Large Letters*, 13.
6. Reece, *Paul's Large Letters*, 14.
7. Richards, *Paul and First-Century Letter Writing*, 169. Rex Winsbury notes that to acquire a good quality composition it cost twenty-five denarii for one hundred lines. For a second quality composition and for the same number of lines it cost twenty denarii (*Roman Book*, 20).

Ephesians which would mean that it cost about one hundred and twenty eight dollars for supplies and a secretary.

LECTORS

Few people could manage public reading in early Christian communities. Scholars believe that the overall level of literacy in the first-century New Testament world was about twenty percent among men and a lower rate for women and those living in the provinces.[8] For the most part, reading was considered physical labor and carried little or no status. Pliny the Younger, who could read, spoke of hiring one of his slaves, who was a slightly better reader than himself, to publicly recite his poetry for him (*Epistulae* 9.34). The congregations likely included both slaves and slave owners. Those slaves who were clerks may have been literate.[9] Other literate groups included scribes, priests, Pharisees, Sadducees, and other religious teachers who provided the masses with access to the holy texts (e.g., Matt 12:3, 5; 19:4; 21:16, 42; 22:31). Trained readers called lectors might have read the letters in the congregation. Or it is possible that someone from the church community would have fulfilled the lector function and been able to read Jude's letter once it arrived.[10]

---

8. There is some debate on the literacy level in the first-century biblical world. In his extensive study of ancient literacy, William V. Harris concludes that the overall level of literacy in the first century ancient eastern Mediterranean world was below fifteen percent (*Ancient Literacy*, 267). Catherine Hezser believes that the literacy rate among Jewish individuals may have been as low as three percent, depending on how one understands and defines "literacy" (*Jewish Literacy*, 496). Based on his study of first century communal reading events, Brian J. Wright contends that written texts were experienced broadly by people of various social and educational levels. This might suggest that the low percentages of literacy among the Roman and Jewish population in the first century was much higher (*Communal Reading*). See also Porter and Pitts, *Fundamentals*, chapter 3.

9. Cf. Plutarch, *Crassus* 2.5–6.

10. For a full discussion of lectors in the early church see De Feo, "Critical Analysis," 297–335.

Letters, Lectors, Performance, and Presence

Ancient manuscripts were not easily sight-read. The punctuation, headings, and paragraphs that cue the modern reader to the proper interpretation of a passage are absent in ancient Greek writing. Vocalization of ancient Greek texts required navigating through a "river of letters"—uninterrupted and unpunctuated streams of capital letters.[11] Slips in speech were criticized by relentless public.[12] The Qumran community was particular about the quality of the public readings of their sacred texts: "And anyone whose {speech} is too soft (?) or speaks with a staccato voice not dividing his words so that {his voice} may be heard, none of these shall read from the book of the Law, lest he cause error in a capital matter" (4 Q226 fragment 5.ii).[13] Thus, a speaker would need to be well acquainted with the work prior to standing before listeners to recite it, dedicating some time to regular practice (Plutarch, *Demosthenes* 8).[14] Further, Quintilian believed that lectors that were going to publicly read a manuscript should read thoroughly over them, examine them carefully, and read them over repeatedly before reciting them to a listening audience (Quintilian, *Institutio oratoria* 10.1.21).

NEW TESTAMENT LETTERS AS PERFORMANCE

New Testament writers were conscious of their letter's reanimation upon arrival at its destination when it was recited in another's voice.[15] Authors whose compositions were to be read aloud knew

---

11. The paleographer Paul Saenger wrote a book focused on Medieval Latin texts that used scriptura continua. He found that scriptura continua made people read slowly and was suitable for reading aloud (Saenger, *Space Between Words*).

12. Lucian, *Slip of the Tongue in Greeting*, 1; Plautus, *Bacchides* 432–34; Irenaeus, *Against Heresies* 3.7.1–2; Petronius, *Satyricon* 68.

13. As noted by Snyder, *Teachers and Texts*, 146.

14. Winsbury, *Roman Book*, 113. However, Jan Heilmann contends we should not assume that reading unspaced scripts was any more cognitively challenging for ancient readers than reading spaced scripts is for us ("Reading Early New Testament Manuscripts.")

15. Reece, *Paul's Large Letters*, 38. The letter may have been supplemented

that people understood the full meaning of a written text by experiencing it being animated or performed. A member of the early church would not only hear the words spoken, but they could also experience the characteristics of the speaker's voice such as modulation, tone, and volume. All these vocal features helped to convey the written or memorized message. There was also a visual component in the delivery of the text. The speaker's facial expressions, body movement, and gestures also enhanced and contributed to the words spoken. Further, audience response and participation were expected and often encouraged during the oral recitation of New Testament literature (e.g., Matt 12:46–50; Mark 6:2–3; Luke 4:20–28; 11:14–28; 1 Cor 14:16). Consequently, New Testament letters did not fully come to life until they were performed before a live audience, using the appropriate and intended vocal variation and physical expression.

To obtain the most convincing argument, lectors or readers might have borrowed some of the tactics of professional speakers and adapted them for their public recitations. The techniques of the professional speaker set the standard for all kinds of public speech. This would have involved the ability to correctly pronounce terms, clearly articulate vocal expressions, pausing at appropriate places in the text, and correctly pronouncing syllables (cf. Irenaeus, *Against Heresies* 3.7.1–2). In the previous citation, the second century bishop Irenaeus, expressed his criticism of a poor lector who reads using inaccurate phrasing and improperly pausing at places in the text. Consequently, the lector unwittingly communicates a heretical theology to the whole community as he reads.[16]

Clues for a reader to use an animated voice, gestures, and encourage audience engagement are sometimes embedded in the texts. Heightened forms of communication marked the Apostle Paul's correspondence with the churches. For instance, his letters included dramatic, rhetorical, and emotional elements to foster

---

by oral expositions by the letter carriers (cf. Josephus, *Jewish Antiquities* 17.133; 20.10; *Jewish War* 4.228–229, 233).

16. Nässelqvist, *Public Reading*, 88.

his teaching (Gal 5:12). The letter of Jude is similarly dramatic, containing intense vocabulary and a lively tone. Even in the short letter of Jude, a range of emotions are mentioned—love or beloved (vv. 1, 2, 17, 20, 21), harshness (v. 15), fear (vv. 12, 22), and hate (v. 22). It is hard to imagine the reader of Jude's passionate letter speaking in a monotone voice and without utilizing his or her hands occasionally for emphasizing portions of his message.

We do not possess any videos to show us what it looked like for someone to perform the New Testament letters to the early church. There are no audio recordings letting us hear the voice of the speaker reading Jude's letter. If we want to learn how ancient readers spoke and what it was like to listen to them, we must rely on clues in the written texts.

In addition to those devices previously mentioned (alliteration, homoeoteleuton, triads, an antiphonal doxology), there are several other types of clues in Jude, which imply the author composed his letter knowing that it would be reanimated by a reader to a listening audience. For instance, places in the text where the author uses second person plural pronouns (Jude 3) and verbs (Jude 17), indicate the author is directly addressing the audience. Allusions to prior events and other written or spoken works are often employed by writers for turning a passive audience into an active one (e.g., Jude 5–8, 14, 23).

LETTERS AS AUTHORIAL PRESENCE

The lively and dramatic nature of the reading of New Testament letters functioned to create a sense of the author's presence. In oral cultures the spoken word performed was often perceived to function as a substitute for an absent author's personal presence. In a correspondence written by the philosopher Seneca, he articulated how ancient people regarded letters as the tangible presence of an absent author. He wrote, "Whenever your letters arrive, I imagine that I am with you, and I have the feeling that I am about to speak my answer, instead of writing it."[17] The Apostle Paul expressed his attendance with the Corinthian congregation through his letter when he stated, "For though absent in body, I am present in spirit; and as if present I have already pronounced judgment in the name of the Lord Jesus on the man who has done such a thing" (1 Cor 5:3–4).

The letter was considered by some ancient rhetorical theorists as one half of a conversation or a replacement for dialogue (e.g., Demetrius, *De elocutione* 223; Cicero, *Epistulae ad familiares* 12.30.1). Seneca conveyed this notion when he wrote, "Whenever your letters arrive, I imagine that I am with you, and I have the feeling that I am about to speak my answer, instead of writing it" (Seneca, *Epistulae morales* 67.2).[18] The words were a mirror of their spoken counterpart, letting the absent author come to life.[19] The author was regarded as concretely present in the reading or hearing of his letter, almost seen and heard through his written words. This notion is expressed in another one of Seneca's letters, "I see you, my dear Lucilius, and at this very moment I hear you; I am with you to such an extent that I hesitate whether I should not begin to write you notes instead of letters. Farewell" (Seneca, *Epistulae morales* 55.11).[20]

Letters, despite their written nature, also brought a material presence of the absent writer through the impress of the hand on the paper (Seneca, *Epistulae morales* 40.1) and through physical contact by the recipient with the letter that was handled by the author.[21] Pliny related this thought when he said, "You say that you are feeling my absence very much, and your only comfort when I am not there is to hold my writings in your hand and often put them in my place by your side" (Pliny, *Epistulae* 6.7.1–3).[22]

---

17. Seneca, *Epistulae morales* 66–92, 37.

18. Seneca, *Epistulae morales* 66–92, 37. See also Cicero (*Epistulae ad Atticum* [177] 9.10.1; *Epistulae ad Quintum fratrem* 1.1.45).

19. Fögen, "Ancient Approaches," 61.

20. Seneca, *Epistulae, Volume I: Epistles* 1–65, 371, 373.

21. Cambron-Goulet, "Orality in Philosophical Epistles," 151.

22. Pliny the Younger, *Epistulae, Volume I: Books* 1–7, 411.

Likewise, Jude's epistle served as a substitute for his personal presence. The lector reciting Jude effectively eliminated the distance in time and space between the author and the reader/audience, giving the author's words real immediacy.[23] The reader of Jude's brief, but powerful letter becomes the author's means of being present in the Christian community. This presence is embodied by the lector who has at his disposal both his body and his voice to deliver the words to the church in the most persuasive and authoritative manner while serving as Jude's substitute. Considering the vocal and bodily expression used in oral presentations, the lector functioned much like a performer.

---

23. Holland, "'Frightening You with Letters,'" 4.

4

Approach of this Commentary

Given the discussion in the previous chapters of the oral and performative nature of the New Testament documents, likely recited by a skilled or well-prepared reader, an oral/performance analysis is a fitting method to analyze Jude and other New Testament literature.[1] In studying a text through the lens of orality and performance one needs to be sensitive to clues in the literature reflecting certain conventions of orally delivered material. Those conventions are: 1) the narrative and rhetorical[2] style of the text, which can direct the audience to important thematic elements, arouse their emotions, and solicit their involvement in the oral performance; 2) and aspects of delivery which include, but are not

---

1. In academia this type of analysis is called performance criticism. For examples of studies that apply biblical performance criticism to New Testament texts, see Shiner, *Proclaiming the Gospel*; Iverson, "Centurion's 'Confession,'" 329–50; Hearon, "Characters in Text and Performance," 53–79; De Waal, *Aural Performance Analysis*; Oestreich, *Performance Criticism*, esp. 152–83; Perry, *Insights*, esp. 173–84; Seal, "Performance Critical Analysis," 243–53.

2. In practice, rhetoric entails the use of a definite and clearly definable artistic strategy that aims through conventional but skillfully employed means of argumentation to modify (that is, to reinforce, modify, or change) the cognitive, emotive, and/or volitional stance of the intended audience. Biblical rhetoric is first and foremost the art of persuading individuals and communities to view the world from God's perspective.

Approach of this Commentary

limited to, voice and gesture.[3] Each of these conventions focuses on one of three elements: 1) someone speaking, 2) someone hearing, and 3) a text.[4] A oral/performance analysis attempts to appreciate these and other conventions of orally performed texts—features often neglected or only briefly mentioned in other commentaries.

In the next chapter, an explanation of the text will follow a translation of each section of the letter of Jude. In addition, Jude will be explored in terms of the interaction of the three performance elements discussed above (the oral rhetorical style of the text, the speaker, and the audience). Further, the footnotes, in addition to providing bibliographic and other helpful information, will identify, and at times comment on, the major textual variants in the manuscripts used to translate Jude from Greek to English. Footnotes will also mark areas in the text where translators have had difficulty understanding the author's intent in the original language. Finally, at places in the text where performance features are identified, there will be some brief comments on present day application of those passages for the church and her members.

---

3. See Whitney Shiner's detailed discussion of these conventions ("Oral Performance of the New Testament," 49–63).

4. Perry, *Insights*, 1. Perry adds a fourth element to consider, the social situation. I merged this with the category of those hearing (the audience) who each have a social situation, which effects how they hear the story.

5

COMMENTARY ON JUDE

TEXT: JUDE 1-2

1 Jude, a servant of Jesus Christ and brother of James,
To those who are called, who are beloved in[1] God the Father
and kept safe for[2] Jesus Christ:
2 May mercy, peace, and love be yours in abundance.[3]

---

1. This preposition could be translated as it is here, "beloved in God," stressing the context where the love is experienced—in fellowship with God. Or it could be translated as "beloved by God," emphasizing God as the agent or source of the love experienced (so NIV). However, Simon J. Kistemaker is correct to note Christians living in the sphere of God's love (in fellowship with him) are consequently loved by God (*James,* 367).

2. The Greek could be translated either ("by Jesus Christ," NIV) or ("for Jesus Christ," NRSV). The latter is the more natural way of reading the Greek. The language implies that God was keeping Christians safe and guarding them until Jesus would gather them when he returned to commence his reign on earth.

3. All biblical quotations are from the NRSV unless otherwise noted.

Commentary on Jude

EXPLANATION OF THE TEXT: ADDRESS AND BLESSING

JUDE BEGINS HIS LETTER with two self-designations. He is a servant of Jesus Christ and a brother of James (v. 1).[4] Next, the recipients are addressed by their Christian identity. They are called, beloved in God, and kept safe for Jesus (v. 1).[5] The three-fold description accentuates how much salvation is entirely of God—it is because of his sovereignty, love, and power.[6] The idea of a divine calling is derived from the Old Testament (Isa 41:9; 42:6; 48:12, 15; 49:1; 54:6; cf. also Hos 11:1), where two forms of calling are spoken of, the choosing of Israel, and the choosing of individual Israelites, or bodies of Israelites.[7] The apostles of Jesus also received a divine calling (Matt 4:21; Mark 1:20). In Jesus's parables, there is the call to enter the kingdom of God, represented by the invitation to a marriage feast (Matt 22:3–9, 14; Luke 14:16–24; cf. Rev 19:9). The calling and the choosing imply each other. The calling is the outward expression of the prior choosing.[8] Jude's recipients have accepted the call to be citizens of God's kingdom and subjects under his rule. Consequently, they experience the love of God and are kept safe for Jesus's return.

The final part of the letter opening is a blessing. While Jude does not direct the prayer to God specifically, the use of the theological passive *plēthyntheiē* (be yours in abundance) indicates that Jude desires God to grant abundant favor to the recipients (cf. Gal 1:3; 1 Tim 1:2; 2 *Baruch* 78:2).[9] He knew that only God could bring about these virtues in the lives of people.[10] In addition to

---

4. For a larger discussion of the author's identity see the Introduction.

5. In other New Testament letters, either specific individuals were addressed (e.g., Philemon, Timothy, Titus), churches (e.g., Corinth, Philippi), or general regions (e.g., Galatia, Asia Minor, the diaspora).

6. Wheaton, "Jude," 1275.

7. Mayor, "General Epistle of Jude," 254.

8. Mayor, "The General Epistle of Jude," 253–54.

9. Watson, *Invention, Arrangement*, 42.

10. Schreiner, *1, 2 Peter, Jude*, 432.

requesting God's abundant mercy, peace, and love, Jude's goal in the prayer was to express his feelings of care and concern for the recipients.

Sending a letter in the ancient world was not a trivial matter, but a clear statement expressing the author's care and compassion for the recipients (cf. Seneca, *Ad Lucilium* 59.1). According to Pseudo-Demetrius (*De elocutione* 224) a letter is "written and sent as a kind of gift."[11] While it was not possible for Jude to be with the Christian community, he dedicated time, energy, and finances[12] to demonstrate his concern for them and their church.

ORAL AND PERFORMANCE FEATURES: STYLE, ĒTHOS, AUDIENCE ENGAGEMENT AND EMOTIONS

The beginning of Jude follows the form "X to Y" that was typical of Jewish letters in which the opening normally named the sender and the recipient(s). This form likely originated in an earlier type of communication where a messenger orally delivered a dispatch to a recipient.[13] When a messenger arrived at the recipient's location he would say, "Thus says X (sender) to Y (recipient)" or other similar forms of verbal introduction (e.g., Acts 15:23; 23:26; Jas 1:1). This type of greeting formula in Jude was a reminder that the author was not physically present with the congregation.

The letter would have been delivered by the hand of a messenger or messengers, from the author who was living in one place, to the recipients' church located elsewhere. Jude may also have assigned a delegate to deliver and read the letter (cf. Rom 16:1-2; Phil 2:25-29). In Jude's absence, his letter would be recited to the gathered community. A lector would act as an intermediary between the author and the audience.

---

11. As cited by Cambron-Goulet ("Orality in the Philosophical Epistle," 154, 155).

12. See the chapter 3 for a discussion of the estimated cost to compose the letter of Jude.

13. Klauck and Bailey, *Ancient Letters*, 18.

As someone who would have read aloud works of history, poetry, biography, and other literature, the lector in antiquity was viewed as someone with considerable authority.[14] Further, it was believed that those who were eloquent in speech had been endowed with communication gifts from the gods or they possessed a divine nature. Odysseus stated about the eloquent orator, "The god sets a crown of beauty upon his words, and men look upon him with delight, and he speaks on unfalteringly with sweet modesty, and is conspicuous among the gathered people, and as he goes through the city men gaze upon him as upon a god" (Homer, *Odyssey* 8.169-173).[15] The orator Cicero claimed divine inspiration of the works by the Greek poet Archias (*Pro Archia* 8.18).

In the opening verse, to establish his own authority, Jude employs rhetorical techniques found in a typical speech of his day.[16] This is especially true in his appeal to *ēthos*, where the attempt is made to establish credibility with his listening audience. Jude's audience would have been more easily persuaded by someone they trusted (Aristotle, *Rhetoric* 1.2.3-4; Quintilian, *Institutio oratoria* 4.1.7). Establishing credibility was important in the opening and closing sections of a discourse (Aristotle, *Rhetoric* 3.19; *Rhetorica ad Alexandrum* 1436a. 33-37). Establishing *ēthos* early in the letter would have given the audience a reason to pay attention to the rest of the epistle.

Jude's designations as both a servant of Jesus Christ[17] and a brother of James served to establish his *ēthos* with the community. The label "servant of Jesus Christ" identified followers of Jesus who had leadership roles in the early church: Paul (Rom 1:1; Gal 1:10; Phil 1:1; Titus 1:1), James (Jas 1:1), and Peter (2 Pet 1:1).[18] The

---

14. Miller, *Performances of Ancient Jewish Letters*, 92.
15. Homer, *Odyssey, Volume I*, 285.
16. Painter and deSilva, *James and Jude*, 190-91.
17. "Christ" is a title meaning one anointed by God.
18. Jerome Neyrey states that the less prominent brother is identified in relation to the more prominent brother, a cultural phenomenon rooted in the Bible (Gen 10:21; Exod 4:14; Josh 15:17; 1 Sam 14:3) and in the general ancient culture (*2 Peter, Jude*, 44).

term has a strong Old Testament background where it is used of servants of God (Abraham [Ps 105:42], Moses [Neh 9:14], David [Ps 89:3]). Jude is using a stereotyped phrase, indicating his authority is the authority of one who represents Jesus.[19]

Further, Jude's description of himself as "brother of James," would have also enhanced his *ēthos*. James was likely known by the recipients for he held a prominent leadership position in the early church (Acts 15:13–21; 21:18; Gal 1:19, 2:9; Eusebius, *Ecclesiastical History* 2.1.2). He also wrote a letter contained in the New Testament. Mentioning his relationship to James makes sense only if the brother is well known to the recipients.[20] Noting his role as a divine servant and his relationship with an established leader of the church was effective because Jude's listeners should trust him to have integrity and, therefore, believe what he says to be true.

In addition to an audience's perception of a respected lector and author, the presence of the physical letter may have symbolically enhanced the reader's authority.[21] How material texts could serve to enhance one's credibility is illustrated in the following quotation. In these passages, Galen, the early second century physician, gives detailed directions to an individual on how to use the physical text as evidence for his argument.

> But you, so that you do not get confused, take up the book of Archigenes and read it to them, first the part having this title for the chapter heading *On the Size of the Heart Beat*. Next, rolling the book up a bit, read again the section *On Intensity* [of the heart beat]. Now roll the book up a little [more] and read the beginning of the section *On Fullness* [of blood in the arteries]. Then, halting the argument for a moment, that is, halting your reading of the book, say to them that I am saying nothing new, but what Archigenes has said too. (*De differentiis pulsuum* 8.591–92K)[22]

---

19. Davids, *Letters of 2 Peter and Jude*, 34–35.
20. Neyrey, *2 Peter, Jude*, 47.
21. Miller, *Performances of Ancient Jewish Letters*, 92.
22. This citation is adapted from Johnson, *Readers and Reading Culture*, 95.

Commentary on Jude

Note how Galen instructs his interlocutor to deploy the manuscript by rolling and unrolling it to the appropriate place in the text and then having him recite the passage to support that his argument is based on an authoritative source.[23] Similarly, as Jude's recipients observed the physical letter being spoken by the reader, its message and instructions gained credibility.

Additionally, a marked performance stylistic feature is evident in the first two verses, which is aimed at capturing the audience's attention and for adding a certain dignity to the letter opening. This feature demonstrates that Jude has a proclivity for triplets. Verses 1 and 2 contain four of at least twenty sets of three that are present throughout the letter.[24]

> Jude, Jesus, James
> Servant, (the) Christ, brother
> Called, beloved, kept
> Mercy, peace, love

Jude's use of four triplets in the address creates a rhythm that has the effect of adding a certain dignity to the letter. Pseudo-Longinus, in discussing the sublime or that which produces exalted language and has the effect of being dignified and filled with grandeur, points to the aural effects of rhythm (*De sublimitate* 39–42).

In addition to creating a dignified opening, the frequency of the trios was helpful for drawing in and keeping the attention of his audience.[25] Jude employs triplets throughout the letter. Their

---

23. Johnson, *Readers and Reading Culture*, 95.

24. Some of the other triplets include: People who left Egypt—Angels who did not keep position—Sodom/Gomorrah (vv. 5–7); defile—reject—slander (v. 8); Cain—Balaam—Korah (v. 11); ungodly—ungodly—ungodly (v. 15); worldly—devoid of the Spirit—causing divisions (v. 19); have mercy—save—show mercy (vv. 22–23). For a discussion and complete listing of triplets in Jude, see Charles, "Literary Artifice," 122–23.

25. In the quote that follows, Cicero exemplifies this technique, "What shall I say about Prodicus of Ceos or [what shall I say about] Thrasymachus of Chalcedon or [what shall I say about] Protagoras of Abdera? each of whom both lectured and wrote what was considering their period a great amount on natural science as well" (*De oratore* 3.128–129, 101). As noted by Michael R.

periodic reemergence encouraged the congregation to get caught up in and anticipate future occurrences of the pattern, which tends to evoke a sense of "collaborative expectancy" within the congregation.[26] Rhythm creates anticipation, a demand for something to come.[27]

Richard Wallaschek explains the power of expectancy in rhythm with the example of someone walking down a road, tapping every lamp post or fence post.[28] If for any reason one of the taps is left out, an emptiness is felt, which can be unpleasant. The nervous system has put itself into a position of expectancy and is ready for the appropriate discharge at the right moment. If the opportunity for the discharge is absent, the gathered energy must disperse itself by other means, which involves a certain amount of conflict and waste. This is the reason a person craves for a rhythmical succession. Jude's triplets are rhythm-creating elements, which sets up in the hearer an expectation that can be satisfied or frustrated.[29]

Three performance elements are present in the blessing. First, New Testament blessings usually follow a typical pattern. The use of "grace, mercy and peace" is found in three letters (1 Tim 1:2; 2 Tim 1:2; 2 John 3), and "grace and peace" is found in three letters (1 Pet 1:2; 2 Pet 1:2; Rev 1:4). Thus, it appears that some combination of these three was the normal Christian letter greeting/blessing. However, while Jude does use mercy and peace, his use of the term "love" is novel—it does not appear in any other New Testament letter blessing.[30] Once established, typical styles, such as the formal blessing of "grace, mercy, and peace," make deviations

---

Cosby (*Rhetorical Composition*, 56).

26. The phrase "collaborative expectancy" is from Roy Jeal (*Integrating Theology*, 84).

27. Uniform runs of repeated elements are not inherently rhythmic, at least not without variation.

28. Wallaschek, *Primitive Music*, 233–34.

29. Dobbs-Allsopp, *On Biblical Poetry*, 109.

30. Not too much should be made of the absence of "grace" in the blessing, since mercy includes the idea of grace (Schreiner, *1, 2 Peter, Jude*, 432).

from the norm stand out. Jude has done this in the use of "love" in his blessing. Deviations can be recognized easily, and the variation becomes significant. Repetition with variation was recommended in the rhetorical handbooks (cf. *Rhetorica ad Herennium* 4.42.54). By using a variation, Jude wanted to draw special attention to God's love, making sure his listeners reflect on this perfection of God.

Second, while reciting the blessing, the reader/performer may have taken on the persona of Jude, embodying the emotional nature of the prayer for God's blessing on the recipients (v. 2). While the blessing would have been spoken in a respectful tone it would have not been delivered deadpan. The prayer language takes the form of a speech-act,[31] which here, when uttered, was to affect the situation of Jude's listeners, entreating that they may receive in abundance, God's blessing of mercy, peace, and love.

Finally, prayers, especially at the beginning of a homily or speech, create a mood of solemnity. Prayers and invocations, among other effects, serve the author's purpose to invite his recipients to remember that God is present at their gathering. Perhaps Jude also wanted the audience to envisage themselves as being constantly watched and/or evaluated by God. The unspoken purpose of reminding the listeners of the divine presence is to instill either fear or encouragement in a person depending on one's relationship with God.

APPLICATION OF THE TEXT

As noted, one of the striking features in this letter opening is the author's use of triads. Jude employs triplets four times in two verses to obtain and sustain the attention of his audience. As a brother of

---

31. Speech-act theory explores how words, both written and spoken, endeavor to change the reader or listener in some way rather than passively communicating ideas. Speech-act theory also proposes that some spoken or written words, rather than simply naming facts, also actually construct a reality. For example, when a minister pronounces a couple as "husband and wife" a change occurs. Only after the pronouncement does the couple officially become married. For a discussion on the relevance of speech-act theory for biblical interpretation see Briggs, "Speech-Act Theory," 75–110.

James and a servant of Christ, Jude has established his credibility and authority as a source for offering genuine divine instruction. However, by mentally priming his audience for future recurrences of this triple pattern, he is securing their attention because what he is about to share in the rest of the letter is more than human advice, but rather divine instruction and wisdom. Jude desires his audience to listen carefully to God's message for them.

As an inspired and canonized text, Jude is also divine wisdom and instruction to modern readers and listeners, which deserves our focused attention. It is a very dangerous thing to not pay attention when God is speaking (when the Word of God is being read), to let one's mind wander and to ignore what is being said. It is the beginning of rebellion when we fail to listen to God.[32] We should make sure our heart is not filled with distractions so that there is no room to receive something worthwhile.

Listening is more than an acoustical function. Listening to anything, including the Bible, can involve only hearing and not lead to any physical or mental change by a listener. Listening is important to ongoing spiritual maturity—one must know what God wants before he or she can do it.[33] The words of God are to be translated into deeds.[34] However, we are often deaf to words that challenge our pride, command our obedience, interrupt our fantasies, or point out our lapses.[35]

Attention to Scripture is vital because it is the sole source for finding out if what we are doing is godly. It is where we find out if what we are doing is ungodly, and where we hear the promises of God and are encouraged. We need all three, affirmation, correction, and motivation.[36] Hearing goes beyond merely letting

---

32. For two good resources on listening and responding to preaching see Leach, *Responding to Preaching*, and Ash, *Listen Up!* Of course, Scripture must be read in an engaging manner to secure and maintain listeners' attention. For help reading the Bible dramatically see Seal and Partridge, *Performing Scripture*.

33. Baker, *Personal Speech-ethics*, 101.

34. Baker, *Personal Speech-ethics*, 102.

35. Peterson, *Reversed Thunder*, 49.

36. Peterson, *Reversed Thunder*, 53.

the sound waves enter the ears, but to hearing that is attentive, responsive, and retentive.

Finally, Jude's emphasis on divine love in the blessing is a reminder that this perfection of God, like all his perfections, is important to consider more often than we do. Divine love is God expressing emotion and "putting himself at risk" in loving people.[37] Some people will never love back—the best will only return that love partially and occasionally. People fall in and out of love. However, God's love stops for nothing, it is resolute and devoted to the other, no matter how far away and hostile the other may be. God's love is one that for which no sacrifice is too great to enrich people who did not ask for it or even opposed it.

TEXT: JUDE 3-4

> 3 Beloved, while eagerly preparing[38] to write to you about the salvation we share, I find it necessary to write and appeal to you to contend for the faith that was once for all entrusted to the saints. 4 For certain intruders have stolen in[39] among you, people who long ago were designated for this condemnation as ungodly, who pervert the grace of our God into licentiousness[40] and deny our only Master and Lord, Jesus Christ.[41]

37. This section relies on Crawford, unpublished "Notes for Systematic Theology," 514.

38. The Greek translated here as "preparing" has caused much debate. Many translators render the phrase as "while eagerly preparing," which suggests that Jude is writing one letter here to accomplish both a discussion of their shared salvation and to encourage them to contend for the faith. Other translators have "although I was very eager to write," (so NIV), which suggests that Jude changed his mind and is writing a different letter to urge them to contend for the faith rather than discuss the salvation they share.

39. "Stolen in" suggests that the intruders were from outside the church and likely a group of itinerant teachers or prophets.

40. "A license for immorality" (NIV). The word (*aselgeia*; licentiousness) often denotes sexual sin (Wisdom of Solomon 14:26; Rom 13:13; 2 Cor 12:21; Gal 5:19; Eph 4:19) or a gross depravity (Mark 7:22; 1 Pet 4:3; 2 Pet 2:2, 7, 18).

41. The ESV translation identifies the ungodly more clearly in verse 4: "For

JUDE

EXPLANATION OF THE TEXT: OCCASION OF THE LETTER

Jude 3-4 introduces the letter's purpose, describing a stealthy invasion by outsiders that has transpired within the recipients' Christian community. Saying the intruders entered the church stealthily indicates it is unlikely that the audience had previously recognized these people as dangerous. Thus, the letter was written to alert them to this reality.[42] This incursion requires them to contend for the faith. The noun "faith" here does not refer to the act of believing; rather it is either a reference to the gospel (including its moral implications) as articulated by Paul and others (Rom 6:10; Heb 9:12; 9:26-28; 10:10; 1 Pet 3:18), or "faith" could refer to the doctrinal content of Christian teaching (v. 3).[43]

The phrase "once and for all" seems to suggest that the doctrinal teaching of the early church had been significantly codified. The effort Jude expected his listeners to utilize in contending for the doctrines of the faith can be discerned based on the Greek term translated as "contend." It is a word that means to exert intense effort against an opponent or on behalf of a person or thing which one depends—it is an action dedicated to the welfare of the larger group.[44] Mental effort is required to understand and teach correct doctrine and combat heresy. Moral effort is needed to apply correct doctrine to one's life.[45] The specifics of the assignment to contend for the faith will be fleshed out in the rest of the letter.

To have the intruders' condemnation designated previously (v. 4) likely refers to the examples that follow in verses 5-16, which

---

certain people have crept in unnoticed who long ago were designated for this condemnation, ungodly people, who pervert the grace of our God into sensuality and deny our only Master and Lord, Jesus Christ."

42. Kraftchick, *Jude & 2 Peter*, 30.

43. Specific Christian teaching that is suggested in the letter include the lordship of Christ (v. 4), grace (v. 4), divine keeping (vv. 1, 6, 13, 24), final judgment (vv. 14-15), and the mercy of the Lord Jesus Christ (v. 21). (Donelson, *I & II Peter and Jude*, 174).

44. BDAG, "ἐπαγωνίζεσθαι" (*epagōnizesthai*), 356.

45. Wheaton, "Jude," 1275.

do not establish that these intruders' actions and destiny were predicted.[46] Instead, the examples confirm that God has judged similar sins in the past, and thus, the future divine judgment for those sins committed by the intruders is certain. Jude will note later in the letter that the apostles predicted the intruders' arrival (vv. 17–18).

ORAL AND PERFORMANCE FEATURES: ALLITERATION AND EMOTION

The marked alliteration of the initial "p" sound in nine of the Greek words of verses 3–4,[47] exploits sound, draws attention to the epistle's purpose statement, and separates these sentences from the previous elaborate language of the address and blessing (vv. 1–2). This manner of presentation of the threat conveys a sense of urgency. An English translation that captures the force of the alliteration follows.

> Beloved, while eagerly preparing to write to you pertaining to the salvation we share, I find it necessary to write and persuade you to contend for the piety of the faith that was once for all passed on to the saints. For certain intruders have privately entered your community, ungodly people who previously were prescribed for this condemnation, who pervert the grace of our God into licentiousness and deny our only Master and Lord, Jesus Christ.[48]

The Greek indefinite pronoun translated in verse 4 as "certain" ("For certain intruders have stolen in among you") might have been contemptuous and would have been especially discernible in spoken language by a certain tone of voice.[49] The Christian

---

46. Painter and deSilva, *James and Jude*, 193.

47. The nine terms are: *pasan* (all), *poioumenos* (preparing), *peri* (about), *parakalōn* (appeal), *paradotheisē* (entrusted), *pistei* (faith), *pareisedysan* (stolen), *palai* (long ago), and *progegrammenoi* (designated).

48. My translation.

49. Du Toit, "Vilification," 48–49.

writer and bishop Ignatius referred to his opponents as "certain people," noting that their names were not even worth mentioning (*To the Smyrnaeans* 5:1–3).[50] Here is one of many cases in the letter where the identity of the referents is intentionally suppressed, and a pronoun is used disparagingly. It serves as an intentional concealing of the faces of the intruders to portray them negatively as shadowy characters, which would have been enhanced with the appropriate tone of voice.[51]

In addition to the presence of indefinite pronouns, emotional parts of a letter are also potential clues for a speaker to modify his voice in accordance with the mood being expressed. In this portion of the letter, where he recounts the occasion for writing, Jude makes an emotional appeal using the vivid and emotive words "pervert" and "licentiousness" and the phrase "certain intruders have stolen in," which communicates secrecy and bad intent (v. 4).[52] Consequently, horror is incited in listeners as the accumulation of emotional terms leaves them with a magnified impression of the undesirable character of these individuals.[53]

APPLICATION OF THE TEXT

Through alliteration and emotive words, which helps to emphasize his purpose for writing, Jude discloses the high importance he places on the church and his contempt for those who wish to destroy it. Christians should seek to embrace the superior worth Jude places on the community of the redeemed. Many actions (or lack of) and words by Christians today demonstrate a rather low view of the church (e.g., little or no church attendance, no attention to the discovery, development, and use of one's spiritual gifts). People are not at liberty to place their own value or worth on the church of Jesus Christ. The Bible attaches its own value to this God

---

50. Noted by Andrie du Toit ("Vilification," 49). See also 1 *Clement* 59.
51. Du Toit, "Vilification," 48–49.
52. Watson, *Invention, Arrangement*, 46.
53. Watson, *Invention, Arrangement*, 47.

ordained institution by designating the extreme cost paid for its establishment—it is the blood bought church of Jesus Christ (Acts 20:28).

The alliteration also emphasizes Jude's intolerance for teaching that deviates from biblical truth, and it cautions us in the relativistic and pluralistic age in which we live to be on guard against doctrinal error. Even Christians interpret Scripture in a way that leads to doctrines and practices that are not acceptable to God. We tend to misinterpret Scripture to support our pervasion of truth. Rather than let the truth transform us, we change the truth so as not to have to conform to it.

TEXT: JUDE 5-8

> 5 Now I desire to remind you, though you are fully informed, that the Lord,[54] who once for all[55] saved a people out of the land of Egypt, afterward[56] destroyed those who did not believe. 6 And the angels who did not keep their

54. Many manuscripts contain the Greek word for "Jesus" (so ESV) while others read "Lord" (so NRSV). Some scholars understand that "Jesus" is the original reading, and that it refers to the pre-incarnate Christ as the one who rescued the Israelites out of Egypt (cf. 1 Cor 10:4). Still other scholars think the reference to "Lord" is original but view it as a reference to Jesus. Given that the one who delivered the Israelites (v. 5) is the same one who executed punishment on the disobedient angels ("he" in v. 6) it is likely that here also Jude is referring to the Lord God.

55. Manuscripts differ concerning the position of "once *for all*" (*hapax*). The NRSV represents manuscripts that have *hapax* in the subordinate clause in the sense that the Lord "once" saved but "later" destroyed those rescued out of Egypt (so NRSV). But other translations side with the manuscripts where "once" modifies the knowledge that the addressees have received and should be rendered "Now I want to remind you, although you once fully knew it" (so ESV). Here it refers to the addressees' knowledge of the whole tradition given once for all. The textual evidence favors placing the word with the first clause (ESV).

56. The word translated here as "afterward" (*deuteron*), usually means "a second time." Here it is a marker that demonstrates a second action of God (the first action was one of salvation and the second action was one of judgment [Reese, 2 *Peter and Jude*, 44]).

43

own position, but left their proper dwelling, he has kept in eternal chains in deepest darkness for the judgment of the great day.[57] 7 Likewise, Sodom and Gomorrah and the surrounding cities, which, in the same manner as they, indulged in sexual immorality and pursued unnatural lust, serve as an example by undergoing a punishment of eternal fire. 8 Yet in the same way these dreamers[58] also defile the flesh,[59] reject authority, and slander the glorious ones.

EXPLANATION OF THE TEXT: THREE ANALOGIES FROM ISRAEL'S SACRED HISTORY

Verse 5 represents the author's continuation of a major attack on those he perceives to be threatening the very foundation of the church (v. 4). Initially, Jude's assault against these threats involves making three references to Israel's sacred history, which are drawn from the Old Testament and other Jewish traditions. He addresses the recipients in a manner that does not insult their intelligence by noting that what he is about to share, they have heard before. It is not clear if Jude assumes his audience has a general knowledge of their sacred history or if he means that the listeners have received specific instruction on these events on prior occasions.[60] Jude did assume that his listeners had a degree of competence about their sacred history.

---

57. For the reference to the "great day" see Zeph 1:14 and 1 *Enoch* 22:11.

58. By calling his opponents "dreamers" (*enypniazomenoi*) Jude is likely referring to their supposed visionary experiences (cf. Acts 2:17, citing Joel 2:28). In the LXX of Deuteronomy (13:2, 4, 6), the word is used to describe the visions that the false prophets claimed to have received. Another view of dreamers sees the false teachers as dreaming of false security, that is, as denying the final judgment of Jesus (1 Thess 5:3; Jer 27:9; Zech 10:3). Jerome Neyrey notes that "this is how 2 Peter interpreted his false teachers. But nothing in Jude supports this suggestion" (2 *Peter, Jude*, 67).

59. Defiling the flesh is sexual sin (*Sibylline Oracles* 2:279; Shepherd of Hermas, *Mandate* 29:9; *Similitude* 60:2).

60. Reicke, *Epistles of James*, 198.

Jude's first reference recalls the fate of the exodus generation. Despite having dramatically experienced God's powerful deliverance at the Red Sea, the Israelites wavered in their trust when it came time to take possession of the land of Canaan (Num 13–14; Ps 95:7b–11). The entire first generation of adults (those twenty years and older) except Joshua and Caleb, were prohibited from experiencing the promised land because they did not trust God to give them the land from the formidable Canaanites (Num 13:25—14:38).

Jude's second example describes the punishment of the angels who did not remain in their proper domain in heaven. They abandoned their position of authority and came to earth to have sexual relations with women (Gen 6:1–4).[61] About two hundred angels, known as the Watchers, left heaven under the leadership of Semyaza and Azazel and cohabitated with human females (1 Enoch 6:1–7). The background for this example comes from Jewish traditions (1 Enoch 6; 7:1; 64:2; 69:5; *Testament of Reuben* 5:6; *Jubilees* 4:22; 5:1).

The final example recounts the punishment of the cities of Sodom and Gomorrah (Gen 18:16—19:29) together with the "surrounding cities" (Deut 29:23). Jude claims that such punishment transpired because the inhabitants of these cities indulged in "sexual immorality"[62] and pursued "unnatural lust" (v. 7b). "Unnatural lust" probably means they lusted after a different order of being (cf. 1 Cor 15:39–40). The inhabitants of these cities sought sexual intercourse with a different order of beings, perhaps angels. If this is

---

61. For a discussion of the various possible identities of the designation "sons of God" in Gen 6:2 see Mathews, *Genesis 1–11:26*, 323–32. One of the proposed identities of the phrase are angels.

62. The verb translated as sexual immorality appears forty-four times in the Septuagint to designate premarital sex (Deut 22:20–21); sex with foreigners (Num 26:1; Philo, *Dreams* 1:89); whoredom or perhaps adultery (Gen 38:24; Hos 1:2, 5); sexual orgies (Hos 4:18); cultic prostitution (Exod 34:15–16; Lev 17:7; 19:9; 20:5; 21:9; Deut 31:16; figuratively as national whoredom (Jer 3:1; Ezek 6:9; 16:16, 20, 26, 28, 30, 33; 20:30; 23:3, 5, 30, 43); and general lusting (Num 15:39; Judg 2:17) (Bateman, "Rebellion and God's Judgment," 462–63).

the case, it serves as a counterpart to the sin of the Watcher angels, who had sexual relations with women.

In this section, Jude recalls numerous examples from Israel's past to help illuminate the fate of the intruders based on the similarities of the sins of both past and current rebels. As Quintilian noted, antiquity exhibits much authority (*Institutio oratoria* 3.7.26).[63] This comparison permits Jude to say "this threat on the church is just like that" in the sense that as God judged rebellion in the past, he will likewise judge these current rebellious individuals at the end of the age (v. 7).[64]

With the phrase, "Yet in the same way also these dreamers" (v. 8), Jude connects the actions of the rebellious individuals more explicitly with the actions of Sodom and the Watchers (who defiled flesh), the Sodomites who alone slandered angels [glorious ones]), and the Sodomites, the Watchers, and the exodus generation who all rejected God's authority.[65]

The dreamers defile the flesh, reject authority, and slander the glorious ones (v. 8). The reference to "defiling flesh" communicates that sexual malpractice was being carried out by the intruders, but the precise nature of this crime is left unexplained. Given that all of Jude's examples rejected divine authority, he undoubtedly had in mind that the intruders also reject the authority of God and/or Christ rather than human authority. The phrase "glorious

---

63. Jim E. Tiles states that people tend to give more validity to tradition the longer they believe it has been handed down by their forebearers. A tradition having been in effect for a long time tends to be something people can live with and can trust (*Moral Measures*, 51–52). Aristotle contended that ancient witnesses were the most reliable since they are unattached to the contemporary situation and therefore were not biased and could not be corrupted (*Rhetoric* 1.15.13–17).

64. Some scholars view the references to the Jewish Scriptures followed by an interpretation in the context of the audience's situation as Jewish Midrash (e.g., Bauckham, *2 Peter, Jude*, 3–5). Midrash is an interpretive technique, which was common among the Qumran community.

65. Painter and deSilva, *James and Jude*, 204. It should be noted that all three sins are attributable to the Sodomites. So, while "yet in the same way," relates generally to all three types, its immediate relation to the Sodomites is appropriate (Bauckham, *2 Peter, Jude*, 55).

ones" probably refers to angels of the court of the God of glory (2 *Enoch* 22:7, 10; Philo, *On the Special Laws* 1.45; Heb 2:2, 9:5),[66] and "slander" (v. 8) likely indicates that the ungodly were speaking disparagingly of angels, who were often represented as enforcing the rule of God (e.g., Isa 37:36; 2 Chr 32:21; 1 Macc 7:41; Susanna 55, 59; Acts 12:23).[67]

ORAL AND PERFORMANCE FEATURES: VOICE

Following Jude's reason for sending the letter, verse 5 opens with "Now (*de*), I desire to remind you . . . " In ancient Jewish letters, the adverb "now" (*de*; *oun*) may have served to indicate a change in volume, tone, or suspense (e.g., 1 Cor 1:10; 11:17; 15:1, 12; 1 Pet 5:1).[68] Because verse 5 begins the exhortation portion of the letter, a tone of confidence and authority would have been appropriate for the reader to project in his voice. In addition, a satirical harsh tone is discernible throughout much of the letter, including verses 5–8, as Jude launches into an extended attack against his opponents.

Whereas a modern reader would usually be satisfied with knowing the intonation that is most appropriate to the passage under consideration, an ancient lector was often expected to reproduce the tone in his delivery.[69] Marginal notes in ancient

---

66. Neyrey, *2 Peter, Jude*, 69.

67. Knight, *2 Peter and Jude*, 45. Jewish belief held that the law of Moses was mediated by angels (*Jubilees* 1:27–29; Josephus, *Jewish Antiquities* 15.136; Acts 7:38, 53; Heb 2:2) and angels made sure it was obeyed (Shepherd of Hermas, *Similitudes* 69:3 [8:3:3]). Slandering could also refer to conduct that was contrary to the law and been considered as "slander" against the angels as guardians of the law.

68. Miller, *Performances*, 117, 132, 139. The adverb "now" (*de*; *oun*) also served to signal to the reader and audience that a different part of the text is being introduced. The adverb would have prepared those listening that the sermon or the teaching and exhortation portion of Jude's correspondence was about to commence. See for example, Jer 29:27 (36:27 LXX); 2 Macc 1:6, 9 LXX.

69. Nünlist, *Ancient Critic at Work*, 349.

manuscripts of dramatic and non-dramatic works appear to aid the reader by providing examples for various aspects of delivery, including the speaker's emotion (e.g., anger, joy, fear), the speaker's attitude (e.g., surprise, spite, irony, sarcasm), the illocutionary force of the utterance (e.g., interrogative, threatening), and its tone (e.g., shouting, with piercing voice, etc.).[70]

By adapting an authoritative harsh tone, the lector would have been able to establish a strong "virtual" presence of Jude in the church community. The individual reciting Jude effectively eliminated the distance in time and space between the author and the reader/audience, giving real immediacy to Jude's words about the sin and punishment of his opponents.[71]

ORAL AND PERFORMANCE FEATURES: RHETORICAL STYLE

It is noteworthy that in the three episodes that Jude asks his recipients to recall, the "oral narrative law of concentration" comes into play (vv. 5–7).[72] Oral narratives concentrate themselves around one main character. This allows the audience to hear what concerns the hero and pay less attention to extraneous details. In the case of Jude's three episodes from Israel's sacred narratives (the exodus, the rebellion of the Watchers, and Sodom and Gomorrah), the main character is God who consistently enacts judgment for disobedience.

Second, Jude uses a rhetorical device called paronomasia or wordplay. Paronomasia is the deliberate choice of two (or more) different words which sound nearly alike (*Rhetorica ad Herennium* 4.21.29–4.23.32; Quintilian, *Institutio oratoria* 9.3.66–67). Wordplay is largely a feature of oral literature because it depends on how words sound. The terms *tērēsantas* ("keep") and *tetērēken* ("kept") sound similar (v. 6). The wordplay highlights the cause and effect

---

70. Nünlist, *Ancient Critic at Work*, 350.
71. Holland, "Frightening You with Letters," 4.
72. Orlik, *Principles for Oral Narrative Research*, 49.

of the angels' disobedience. Because the angels did not keep their heavenly position for the sake of illicit relations with mortal women, God must keep them in perpetual bondage until the day of judgment. In addition to highlighting the cause and effect of sin, wordplay in all its forms was evidence of an author's mastery of language and would have added credibility to Jude's message.

Finally, the use of homoeoteleuton underscores Jude's opponent's sins: *mainousin . . . athetousin . . . blasphēmousin* ("they defile . . . reject . . . slander"; v. 8).[73] Homoeoteleuton is a sound technique that reiterates a series of words or phrases with similar endings, creating a rhythmical effect, thereby highlighting the sin list for Jude's audience (Quintilian, *Institutio oratoria* 9.3.77).

ORAL AND PERFORMANCE FEATURES: EMOTIONS

Emotionally charged language is a component of oral speech and can be more conducive to promoting spiritual formation than propositional statements alone. Thus, meaning is found not only in propositional statements but also in the emotions conveyed and aroused by the text. Jude is expressive literature designed not only to communicate on a rational basis, but also on an emotional one—it is an emotionally charged letter.

During highly emotional occasions, Scripture often portrays individuals quoting or alluding to the Hebrew Bible. For example, in Luke 23:46, Jesus cries out with a loud voice, saying, "Father, into your hands I commend my spirit" (Ps 31:5 [Ps 30:6 LXX], NRSV). In a fervent prayer, the early church recited Ps 2:1 (Acts 4:24-30; cf. Ps 22:1 [21:2 LXX]). Quoting and alluding to numerous Old Testament passages, Peter passionately addressed the crowd who witnessed the dramatic effects of the pouring out of the Spirit (Acts 2:14-36).

When the lector recited/performed the allusions to the Hebrew Bible and other Jewish traditions (vv. 5-7), it might have

73. Bauckham, 2 *Peter, Jude*, 44.

cued him to be more expressive while reading these texts. Both Quintilian, (*Institutio oratoria* 6.2.26), and the author of *Rhetorica ad Herennium* (3.22) stressed the importance for an audience to witness genuine emotions of the speaker as a catalyst to stir the spectators' emotions. Students of public speaking were trained to change their tone with changes in emotions (Cicero, *De oratore* 3.17.56–59; Dionysius, *Demosthenes* 54).

Given the likelihood that verses 5–8 was to be expressed emotionally, it is significant that Jude 5 opens using the first person singular "I" ("Now I desire to remind you..."). Texts that use the first person singular "I" or plural "we" can draw the reader/performer into the script and allow for the harmonization of the emotions conveyed in the text and the emotions of the reader.[74] The use of the first person singular "I" and the second person plural "you" also invites the audience to become a participant in the action.[75] As the lector takes on the persona of Jude, adapting his harsh rhetoric, the passionate indictment against his opponents may have become a self-indictment for some in the listening audience.

ORAL AND PERFORMANCE FEATURES: AUDIENCE PARTICIPATION AND REPETITION

We can observe some of the ways Jude attempted to gain and preserve his listener's interest in verses 5–8. An initial method Jude exploits to gain audience involvement is the reference to material from the Hebrew Bible and other Jewish texts (vv. 5–7). In an oral environment, history was primarily relived through a performative retelling of it because access to the past could not be found in a library.[76] In oral cultures the recollection of traditions was not for the purpose of retrieving data, but for recreating and reliving

---

74. Miller, *Performances*, 85. At the same time, use of the first-person, presents Jude as a knowable and reliable source. Oral cultures tend to accept more willingly what they hear from a known and trusted source (Dinkler, *Silent Statements*, 57).

75. Miller, *Performances*, 169.

76. Shiell, *Reading Acts*, 10–11.

an experience.⁷⁷ Jude's reference to the acts of divine judgment performed in Israel's past was for the purpose of recalling in the collective consciousness of the community how God responded to three examples of disobedience. Noteworthy is that these sacred traditions were familiar to the audience (v. 5). However, Jude proceeds to repeat them. While it is not new information, it is still effective for Jude's purposes. In modern Western cultures, a written text is often only meaningful if it is conveying new knowledge or information.⁷⁸ However, in performances from oral cultures such as the first-century Mediterranean world of Jude, the information shared does not need to be new to be effective. Speakers do much more than just transmit new information or beliefs to their listeners. Instead, speakers, especially those speakers who performed oral epic traditions,⁷⁹ were less concerned with passing on new information and are more interested in reaching a state of mutual involvement or rapport with their addressees.⁸⁰

Therefore, what is important to Jude as he retells events from Israel's past, is the establishment of common ground with his audience. This involves having each listener's mind focused on the same themes and ideas of these traditions.⁸¹ When the idea of divine judgment for sin is active in both the speaker's and audience's minds, it is manifest in a very real sense as a shared experience. Moreover, to retrieve something from the past and bring it to the

---

77. Foley, "Memory in Oral Tradition," 92.

78. Bakker, "Activation," 5–20.

79. The traditions that Jude recalls are epic in the sense that they are three episodes coming from a long historical narrative that contains supernatural elements. They are episodes from the larger epic of the redemptive narrative from the Hebrew Bible and other important Jewish texts, which was important enough to be foundational for the collective experience of the community hearing it. Epics contain a proliferation of episodes and characters, including a hero. The action usually focuses on an epic feat performed by the hero where a battle is won, and a kingdom is established (Ryken, *Words of Delight*, 127–28). God is the hero par excellent who advances his kingdom by punishing disobedience that runs contrary to his mission to provide redemption for humanity.

80. Bakker, "Activation," 8.

81. Bakker, "Activation," 9.

present is to say, "Pay attention to this again. This is still salient; this still has potential meaning."[82]

The threefold reflection on God's punishment of the exodus generation, the Watcher angels and Sodom and Gomorrah (a kind of repetition with variation) also serves to present multiple witnesses that testify to how God deals with rebellion. The three testimonies allow the listener time to process the divine reality, aiding in his or her comprehension of Jude's emphasis in this portion of the letter. Having multiple witnesses also communicates that such widespread testimony is to be taken with due seriousness as it accurately conveys the character of God and the kind of behavior that he abhors.[83]

Verse 6 is a twofold statement that resembles poetic parallelism, which is another feature that can generate audience involvement.[84] By way of grammatical parallelism, Jude describes the angels who rebelled against God in leaving their heavenly abode.[85] Here, an initial adjectival participle "angels who did not *keep*" is followed by a second adjectival participle "but *left*," creating a rhythm of thought, by restating in a structured or systematic way the idea of the angels' abandonment of their dwelling.

> And the angels who did not keep their own domain,
> but left their appropriate dwelling ... [86]

Another example of parallelism appears in verse 7 where Jude describes Sodom's disregard for God's marital norms.[87] The adjectival participles "indulged in sexual immorality" and "pursued unnatural lust" modifies the cities.

82. Kent, *Say It Again, Sam,* 76–77.

83. The validity of testimony was affirmed by two or three witnesses (Deut 17:6; 19:15; John 5:31–33; 8:17–18; Matt 18:16; 2 Cor 13:1; 1 Tim 5:19; Heb 10:2). Jude repeatedly corroborates evidence from a threefold witness.

84. True parallelism, traditionally called "synonymous parallelism," is a twofold statement of a single idea or concept that employs near synonymous or related vocabulary in a symmetrical fashion. "Synthetic parallelism" is a structure in which the second line supplements the first. Antithetic parallelism is identified when parallel statements are placed in opposition to one another.

85. Noted by Bateman, *Jude,* 88.

86. My translation.

87. Noted by Bateman, *Jude,* 88.

As Sodom and Gomorrah and the cities around them
indulged in sexual immorality
and pursued unnatural lust...⁸⁸

Both these examples of parallelism in verses 6 and 7 provide the two verses with a certain rhythm. Listeners may have heard the rhythm generated by the parallelism, allowing them to embody the feelings characterized by the pattern. Rhythm has the potential to bind actor and spectator together. Oliver Sacks states that rhythm turns listeners into participants, makes listening active and motoric, and synchronizes the brains and minds of all who participate.⁸⁹ It is very difficult to remain detached, to resist being drawn into a poetic cadence. Research into the cognitive effects of rhythm suggests that "rhythmic patterns lock in motor responses at the neurological level, and usually produce emotions below the level of consciousness."⁹⁰ As Bruce McConachie states, embodied rhythms involve much more than toe tapping, but that may be one outward expression of the complex neurological and physical response.⁹¹

ORAL AND PERFORMANCE FEATURES: GESTURES

As highlighted in chapter 2, the hands and arms were used by orators to display emotions and to accompany and support them in their verbal communication. One means where hands could be deployed is alongside adverbs and pronouns when there was a need to point out places or persons. Beginning in verse 8, Jude makes extensive use of this last way hands could function, by using one of the many deictic pronouns ("these") present in the letter.

Jude's use of "these" ("Yet in the same way these dreamers..." [v. 8]) ⁹² is significant because the deictic pronoun is very

---

88. My translation.
89. Sacks, *Musicophilia*, 244–45.
90. McConachie, *Engaging Audiences*, 68.
91. McConachie, *Engaging Audiences*, 68.
92. "These" (*houtoi*) is also present in vv. 10, 12, 14, 16, and in v. 19, "them" (*autois*).

likely to have required the use of gesticulation, with a view to turning the gaze of the audience toward an imaginary group of the accused opponents present in the church.[93] In ancient Greek texts such as Homer's *Illiad*, scholars have noted the importance of demonstrative pronouns as potential signifiers of a required or suggested dramatic gesture, which may be performed by the speaker while reciting the pronoun.[94] A demonstrative pronoun, if only heard or read, does not provide the needed direction that the pronoun implies.[95] In the sentence, "these dreamers also defile the flesh, reject authority, and slander the glorious ones" [v. 8]), the pronoun requires a pointing gesture to identify the referent. With the gesture of pointing, the lector can direct attention to an empty space, referred to as *abstract deixis*.[96] However, the space is not empty. While the referents (Jude's adversaries) are abstract, through the application of a pointing gesture, they obtain a degree of physical reality, as if they were present in the church where Jude was being recited.[97]

Taking into consideration that there are indications in the letter that intruders were at times physically present when the church gathered (vv. 4, 12, 19), it is likely that at least some of them were present and heard Jude's letter while it was being read. Bernard Oestreich argues that in the early church, people in the same social group were likely to have sat together.[98] Thus, it is possible that in the context of reading Jude to the gathered church, the lector might have been able to directly address certain sections of the audience where the intruders were sitting and perhaps even gesture to them when referencing them by the pronoun "these." Likely it would have been an effective strategy, but perhaps also a bit adversarial, and so perhaps restrained.

---

93. This section relies on Seal, "Jude Delivered," 93–108.
94. Boegehold, *When a Gesture*, 36–37, 70–71, 112–13.
95. Boegehold, *When a Gesture*, 36.
96. McNeill et al., "Abstract Deixis," 5.
97. McNeill et al., "Abstract Deixis," 5.
98. Oestreich, *Performance Criticism*, 86–113.

Even if the intruders were not present at the reading of the letter, when the lector shifts the orientation "off-stage," through a turning of his or her gaze or gesture of hand, the audience is invited to identify closely with, or even "become," a character (the intruders) in the dialogue for the duration of that address.[99]

APPLICATION OF THE TEXT

One cannot read and fully understand Jude (or the rest of the New Testament) the way the authors (human and divine) intended, by believing that the Old Testament is unimportant or insignificant. Jude, like the rest of the New Testament, has numerous quotations, allusions, and echoes, none of which can be fully grasped apart from some familiarity with the Old Testament.

With the New Testament canon, Scripture is complete, and we now have in whole "the faith that was once for all delivered to the saints" (v. 3). However, this "faith" is only correctly understood within the framework of the whole counsel of God, that includes the entire Old Testament. It is important for Christians to listen to the entire story of God's self-revelation, from creation to the consummation of all things.

Not only did Jude expect his listeners to have been exposed to their sacred texts at some point in the past, but also to remember them. Biblical "remembering" not only recalls the past; it also speaks to the present and the future, helping a person connect previously acquired wisdom to current and future decisions.[100] The events of the past become an aid in the present by producing some activity of the will, the body, or both.

The book of Jubilees teaches that forgetfulness leads to moral corruption and remembrance leads to right action.[101] Jubilees conveys that when Joseph was petitioned by Potiphar's wife, he remembered the words spoken by Abraham and did not lie with

---

99. Whitenton, "Feeling the Silence," 278.
100. Arthurs, *Preaching as Reminding*, 13.
101. Snyder, *Teachers and Texts*, 159.

her. The text states "that there is no man who (may) fornicate with a woman who has a husband (and) that there is a judgment of death which is decreed for him in heaven before the LORD Most High" (Jubilees 39:6).

The opposite of remembering is forgetting, which biblically also implies more than lack of mental recall.[102] Biblical forgetting is equal to "forsaking" and "rejecting" God and his ways (e.g., Deut 8:11, 19; Judg 3:7; Hos 4:6–7). The person who does not forget God, fears him, delights in his statutes, and does not stray from his instructions (Pss 119:16, 109–10).

By bringing the past into the present with compelling power, emotional intensity, and sustained emphasis, Jude does more than inform us and his audience of the fate of the rebellious intruders. He reminds us/them that now or in the future, we/they are in danger of suffering the same punishment if we/they stray into rebellion.[103] Positive responses to divine warnings reveal who really belongs to the people of God.[104]

References to the wilderness generation, the Watchers, and Sodom and Gomorrah convey Jude's belief that God can and does intervene and decisively influence the affairs and experiences of the everyday world.[105] God is sovereign in the past over the heavenly and earthly realms, and he will be sovereign in the future over the condemnation of the false teachers. History is moving toward the day when all evil will be destroyed, and God will reign supreme. The action of all these people, though seemingly contrary to the divine will, were in no way outside the control of God.[106]

Finally, Jude's expressive letter provides some instruction for the preaching and teaching ministries of the church. While argument and explanation in the power of the Holy Spirit clearly play a role in people's conversion and spiritual formation, the emotional intensity in Jude's letter, and the rest of the Bible for that matter,

---

102. Arthurs, *Preaching as Reminding*, 18.
103. Donelson, *I and II Peter*, 180.
104. Schreiner, *1, 2 Peter, Jude*, 447.
105. Joubert, "Facing the Past," 57, n. 2.
106. Joubert, "Facing the Past," 68.

suggests that passion is also needed to support theological claims. Neuroscience affirms the inseparability of thinking and feeling.[107] Preachers and teachers should not manipulate people's emotions into doing what their minds reject but teaching and preaching should also not be dull and empty of emotions. That mode of expression will not reach the heart.

TEXT: JUDE 9-10

> 9 But when the archangel Michael contended with the devil and disputed[108] about the body of Moses, he did not dare to bring a condemnation of slander against him, but said, "The Lord rebuke you!" 10 But these people slander whatever they do not understand, and they are destroyed by those things that, like irrational animals,[109] they know by instinct.

EXPLANATION: ANOTHER ILLUSTRATION OF DIVINE PUNISHMENT FOR SIN

Many scholars believe that Jude's source in verse 9 was the lost ending of the work sometimes known as the *Assumption of Moses*[110] (and/or the *Testament of Moses*),[111] which uses a quote from Zech 3:2 ("The Lord rebuke you, O Satan"). Although the ending

---

107. Novella, *Your Deceptive Mind*, 12. As noted by (Arthurs, *Preaching as Reminding*, 58).

108. Alliteration is present in these three words *diabolō, diakrinomenos, dielegeto* ("Michael dueled with the devil and disputed about the body of Moses" [my translation]).

109. Literally "unspeaking living ones."

110. E.g., Kelly, *Epistles of Peter and of Jude*, 265; Kistemaker, *James*, 9; Watson, *Invention, Arrangement*, 56.

111. Bauckham, *2 Peter, Jude*, 76. R. H. Charles argued that the two works (the *Assumption of Moses* and the *Testament of Moses*) were combined and the whole came to be known as the *Assumption of Moses* (Charles, "Assumption of Moses," 407–8).

of the *Assumption of Moses* is no longer in existence, several sources seem to have preserved the substance of the story it contained. From those sources, a reconstructed outline of the story, which is an expansion of the details of Moses's burial (Deut 34:5-6) is as follows. After Moses's death, God sent the archangel Michael to remove the body of Moses from where it had been buried and take it elsewhere. However, the devil (Samma'el), opposed him, disputing that Moses had no right to an honorable burial because Moses committed murder when he killed an Egyptian and hid his body in the sand (Exod 2:11-15). Because the devil's accusation was slander or blasphemy against Moses, Michael said to the devil, "May the Lord rebuke you, devil!" At that, the devil fled.[112]

It is not entirely clear what Jude was intending to communicate with his reference to Michael's dispute with the devil. There are primarily two views about Jude's intent. The first view considers that Jude's reference to the dispute is a reply to the challenge by the ungodly opponents to the administration of divine law (they "reject authority, and slander the glorious ones," [v. 8]).[113] If Michael the archangel, as one having authority to judge the devil, did not dare to pronounce judgment on him for slander (v. 9b), then the ungodly should not presume they can acquit themselves of the charges that the angels (as administers and guardians of the divine law) direct against their ungodly practices.[114] This interpretation highlights the arrogance of the ungodly, who view themselves as being above the law.

A second interpretation of Jude's point in referencing Michael's dispute with the devil is that it serves to illustrate proper speech ethics and highlights divine punishment for any speech that violates those principles. The term *blasphēmeō* ("slander"; vv. 8, 9, 10) refers to the act of speaking in a disrespectful or irreverent way that demeans, denigrates, or maligns a human or transcendent being.[115] Thus, if Michael the archangel did not resort to

---

112. Reconstruction from Bauckham (*2 Peter, Jude*, 72-73).
113. Neyrey, *2 Peter, Jude*, 66.
114. Painter and deSilva, *James and Jude*, 205.
115. BDAG, "βλασφημίας" (*blasphēmias*), 178.

slander ("slanderous judgment," NET) in dealing with the devil, how much more should the ungodly not engage in slander.[116] Further, the story illustrates that when the intruders do slander, they should expect consequences in the form of divine judgment. Regardless of Jude's point in referencing Michael's dispute with the devil, God judges both the intruders and the devil for their behaviors.

Jude concludes this section by stating that when the opponents follow their own cravings, they degrade themselves to the level of "irrational animals," a downward spiral that leads to their destruction (v. 10). Jude contends that these (all) people lose something of their humanity and are diminished, when they resign to their cravings.[117]

ORAL PERFORMANCE FEATURES: SIMILES

The comparison of the opponents to irrational animals is a simile, which pointed to their lower natures (e.g., 4 Ezra 8:29–30; 4 Macc 14:14, 18). A simile is a verbal comparison where an idea or entity is likened to another idea or entity, which has similar features.[118] The usefulness of the simile for heightening emotion and for creating *pathos* is commonly noted by the scholiasts.[119] In Homer's *Iliad*, similes mark emotional peaks in the narrative.[120] When a listener hears the verbal signal "like" or "just as" they prepare for a comparison exercise and recall the appropriate image.[121]

Similes aid storytellers and audiences in a variety of ways. For example, similes serve storytellers and audiences by explaining and modeling, invoking a fresh understanding of something,

---

116. Green, 2 *Peter and Jude*, 196; Reicke, *Epistles of James*, 202.
117. Painter and deSilva, *James and Jude*, 206.
118. Minchin, "Similes in Homer," 29.
119. Martin, "Similes and Performance," 140. Sources for the ideas of how similes functioned in the ancient world come from scholia (notes by ancient commentators [scholiasts]) to the Homeric poems found in Aristotle.
120. Martin, "Similes and Performance," 144–46.
121. Minchin, "Similes in Homer," 30.

filling gaps when there is not a term to describe an action or behavior (or the storyteller cannot recall one), expressing emotional attitudes, decorating and expressing hyperbole, and by forming a mutual understanding between teller and listener.[122] All of these functions may have been in Jude's mind as he viewed the conduct of the opponents to be as unreasonable as animals and wished to communicate this view with as much passion and intensity as possible.

ORAL PERFORMANCE FEATURES: QUOTATIONS

Verse 9 contains a quotation by the angel Michael when addressing the devil's slander of Moses: "The Lord rebuke you!" Quotations can be considered a type of demonstration. Just as you can demonstrate a golf swing or a person's manner of walking, you can also demonstrate what a person did in saying something. When face to face, people can perform communicative acts by three fundamental methods: indicating, describing, and demonstrating.[123] Demonstrations and descriptions are fundamentally different methods of communication. Demonstrations portray their referents—what is being demonstrated—whereas descriptions do not.[124] When Jude quotes Michael, he is demonstrating the sentence the angel uttered. He can also depict his emotional state (excitement, anger), voice pitch (male), illocutionary act (reprimand, threat), and even the nonlinguistic actions that accompanied his speech (pointing gestures, frown, head angle).

Anna Wierzbicka's "theatrical" theory of quotations is applicable here.[125] The theory posits that in using quotes from others, an author is dramatizing the words of an earlier speaker to a later audience, and thereby temporarily assuming the role of that speaker. As the lector reports Michael's words by quoting them, he

---

122. Minchin, "Similes in Homer," 32–33.
123. Clark and Gerrig, "Quotations as Demonstrations," 765.
124. Clark and Gerrig, "Quotations as Demonstrations," 764.
125. Wierzbicka, "Semantics," 267–307, esp. 272.

temporarily assumes the role of the archangel—imagining himself as the other person. Ancient rhetoricians knew that quotations could enhance speech (Quintilian, *Institutio oratoria* 1.8.10–12; 2.7.4). For Jude, to demonstrate the Michael and the devil event was to reenact or resurrect it. For the listeners, they become engrossed in the event, reexperiencing it vividly, entering the scene as if they were present at the original event.

APPLICATION OF THE TEXT

Angels are mentioned four times in this very short letter (vv. 6, 8, 9, 14). In Jude, they are called glorious ones (v. 8). In addition, Jude reveals that one of the seven elevated positions of archangel of God is held by Michael (v. 9),[126] and that angels are called holy ones that will accompany Christ and execute judgment on humanity at the eschaton (vv. 14–15). While these celestial beings clearly hold a superior position in God's cosmos, they are not allotted divine grace and mercy like humanity. For while Adam sinned, as did all generations after him, the second Adam, in grace and mercy, came to redeem all humanity (Rom 5:12, 19; 1 Cor 15:45). However, angels also sinned (cf. v. 6) but are not offered the same redemption by Christ (Heb 2:16)[127]—a reality worthy of meditation, that focuses on God's special love for people.

This simple yet deeply profound and sobering truth is illustrated by the famous Swiss Reformed theologian Karl Barth. Barth is probably most well-known for his massive, unfinished five-volume summary of theology, *Church Dogmatics* (later published in twelve volumes). During a tour of the United States in 1962, he was asked by a student to recall the most momentous theological discovery he had made during his long life. Barth replied, "Jesus loves me this I know, for the Bible tells me so."[128]

---

126. Michael was one of seven archangels (1 *Enoch* 20).
127. Noted by Kistemaker (*James*, 388).
128. Mangina, *Karl Barth*, 9.

TEXT: JUDE 11-13

11 Woe to them! For they go the way of Cain, and abandon themselves to Balaam's error for the sake of gain, and perish in Korah's rebellion. 12 These are blemishes[129] on your love-feasts, while they feast with you without fear, feeding themselves.[130] They are waterless clouds carried along by the winds; autumn trees without fruit, twice dead, uprooted; 13 wild waves of the sea, casting up the foam of their own shame; wandering stars, for whom the deepest darkness has been reserved forever.

EXPLANATION OF THE TEXT: A WOE ORACLE

Verse 11 takes the form of a woe or lament oracle, a prophetic announcement of judgment on sinners, which is found in both the Old and New Testaments (e.g., Isa 3:9; Hos 7:13; 9:12; Matt 26:24; Mark 13:17).[131] The use of a woe oracle implies a supernatural

---

129. The Greek word the NRSV has rendered "blemishes" could also be translated as "hidden reefs." If so, then the false teachers are like hidden reefs that were a potential hazard to boats. Furthermore, the translation "hidden reefs" fits with the nature imagery that dominates these verses (Donelson, *I and II Peter*, 182).

130. The NRSV renders the Greek *poimainontes* as "feeding" (or pasturing), which also can mean shepherding. So, the ESV and NIV translates the word as "shepherds feeding themselves." Shepherds was used as a metaphor for someone serving in a leadership role (e.g., Ezek 34:1-4; *Martyrdom and Ascension of Isaiah* 3:24; John 21:16; Acts 20:28).

131. The woe oracle developed within and outside the Old Testament. Waldemar Janzen contends that the Hebrew term *hôy* (often rendered in the Septuagint as *ouai* or *oimoi* ["alas" or "woe"]), was rooted in the funeral lament (Janzen, *Mourning Cry*, 27). Janzen notes there is also some strong component of vehement accusation that has led interpreters to seek some association with the curse. Sorrow, mourning, and wailing on the one hand meet with accusation, and curse in the face of violent death, where mourning for the dead shades over into cursing of the one guilty of the death. If someone was a victim of murder, the voice of public justice is often raised over the bier of the dead in the form of the funeral lament. Here mourning becomes accusation, and often the name of the murderer is first heard from the lips of the women mourning

COMMENTARY ON JUDE

prophetic consciousness on the part of Jude. Either Jude himself delivers a prophetic oracle, or he quotes an already existing oracle. Since Jude usually identifies the quotations of others (cf. vv. 14, 17), this prophecy likely derives from Jude, and ultimately from God or Christ.[132]

The woe oracle usually indicates the divine judgment to be precipitated on the guilty (they will perish) and the reason for the judgment (they "go the way of Cain and abandon themselves to Balaam's error for the sake of gain, [they have taken the way of] Korah's rebellion"). Stating as a completed action, that the false teachers have "perished in Korah's rebellion" (v. 11 ESV), is a striking way of saying that their doom is certain and settled. Like the preceding verses (5-7), Jude again refers to three Old Testament examples, which serve as types to the interlopers.

In this series of Old Testament references, it appears that Jude has selected these three individuals because they represent people who have enticed others to sin. Cain (Josephus, *Jewish Antiquities* 1.61; Philo, *On the Posterity of Cain* 38-89), Balaam (Num 24:14, 25; 31:8; Rev 2:14; Philo, *On the Life of Moses* 1.295-300), and Korah (Num 16:1-35; 1 *Clement* 51:3-4) all can be said to be guilty of leading others astray and make the point that Jude's opponents also lead others from the truth. This justifies calling the opponents "false teachers." While we usually consider Cain's murder of his brother Abel as his claim to fame, he was also known in Jewish tradition as one who taught others evil as the following quote reveals: "He [Cain] augmented his household substance with much wealth, by rapine and violence; he excited his acquaintance to procure pleasures and spoils by robbery, and became a great leader of men into wicked courses" (Josephus, *Jewish Antiquities* 1.61).[133]

In verse 12 the false teachers are further described as being present at the community's love feats, partaking in the meal in an inappropriate manner, not regarding its sanctity, and without fear

---

the dead.

132. Watson, *Invention, Arrangement*, 58.
133. Josephus and Whiston, *Works of Josephus*, 31.

of any divine consequences (cf. 1 Cor 11:17–34).[134] Love feasts refer to the ritual celebration of the bread and wine (the Lord's Supper), in addition to a full meal together, which the church enjoyed.

Jude also calls out the false teachers for feeding themselves, perhaps meaning that in doing so they were neglecting those in need. It is not entirely clear if Jude is thinking of the opponents' selfish preoccupation with their own interest in general, or more specifically of their conduct at the love feast. The context and choice of verb *poimainontes* (feeding) make the latter interpretation more probable.[135]

Next, four metaphors, depicting nature in a chaotic state are employed to characterize the false teachers—they are waterless clouds (cf. Prov 25:14), autumn trees without fruit, twice dead, uprooted (cf. Matt 7:16–20), wild waves of the sea (cf. Isa 57:20),[136] and wandering stars.[137] Many Second Temple Jewish writings use the cosmological created order as a model for the order that should exist or should be established in the human realm (cf. 1 *Enoch* 2:1—5:4). A creation poem in 1 *Enoch* depicts the sea at rest on a foundation of sand and the sun, moon, and stars moving according to an established course (69:16–25).[138] Another text states

---

134. An alternative understanding of the term "fear" connects it with shepherds, so that the false teachers are "fearlessly shepherding themselves" (Davids, *Letters of 2 Peter and Jude*, 70).

135. Kelly, *Epistles of Peter and of Jude*, 271.

136. Today the sea is often seen as a thing of beauty; to ancient people, less able to cope with the sea's fury, it was a terror, and many perished in its fury. Revelation 21:1, with its promise of no more sea, reflects this attitude (Blum, "Jude," n.p.).

137. Jude is probably alluding to the Watcher angels who are described as wandering stars, disobedient to God (1 *Enoch* 18:13–16; 21:3–6; 88:1–3; Watson, *Invention, Arrangement*, 63).

138. 1 *Enoch* is a collection of at least seven pieces of work by various authors. These seven works include *The Book of Watchers* (chs. 1–36), *The Book of Parables* (chs. 37–71, also known as the *Similitudes*), *The Book of the Luminaries-Astronomical Book* (chs. 72–82), *The Book of Dreams* (*Animal Apocalypse*; chs. 83–90), *The Epistle of Enoch* (chs. 91–105), *The Book of Noah* (chs. 106–107), and the final work in chapter 108 (often considered an appendix) called *Another Book of Enoch*. These seven sections of 1 *Enoch* represent the evolving phases of the Enochic corpus, which may or may not have been

that God created the stars to fix time from day to day and that they never deviate from their appointed course (*Psalms of Solomon* 18:11-14; Sirach 16:24-30).[139] However, in 1 *Enoch* 80:2-8, nature, which usually is obedient to the natural laws set forth by God, falls into chaos in the last days.[140] In an apocalyptic tone, Jude is comparing the false teachers to nature gone awry at the end of the age.[141] The wicked false teachers likewise transgress God's laws—they are condemned to eternal darkness (v. 13). If light symbolizes God, darkness suggests everything that is anti-God[142] and ultimately symbolizes being separated from him.

Images of punishment were a common feature of apocalyptic literature. For example, the author of 1 *Enoch* demonstrates one such lucid description: "And then in one place the fathers will be smitten with their sons, and brothers will fall in death with one another" (1 *Enoch* 100:1). The ungodly are often portrayed as experiencing fire and torment (e.g., 2 *Baruch* 44:15). Descriptions

---

originally written in this order. The author of 1 *Enoch* is pseudepigraphically identified as the patriarchal figure Enoch found in Gen 5:21-24. The individual works are dated variously.

139. In Gen 1, creation is depicted as obediently responding to a magisterial and in-charge deity whose word is all powerful. By bringing the world into existence by utterance the imagery is that of a powerful sovereign (a king) who utters a decree from the throne and in the very spoken word it is accomplished, done, finished, and obeyed (Niditch, *Oral World*, 11).

140. Watson, *Invention, Arrangement*, 62. The illustrations of the lawlessness of nature given in 1 *Enoch* 80:2-7 include three of Jude's four metaphors, in the same order as in Jude 12-13: rain withheld from the earth (80:2), fruits of the trees withheld (80:3), and, at the end of the passage, the stars drifting from their proper times and orbits (80:6-7). As noted by Bauckham, "Jude's Exegesis," 426.

141. Other themes often associated with apocalyptic literature that are present in Jude include the angels or otherworldly beings mediating revelation (v. 14); the imminent eschatology (v. 18); God's cosmic intervention into human affairs to bring an end to all forms of evil and to execute judgment on all sinners (vv. 14-15); God's intervention on behalf of the faithful on the last day (v. 21).

142. Everything anti-God can include the wicked (Prov 2:13-14; 1 Thess 5:4-7) and death (Ps 88:12). Salvation brings light to those in darkness (Isa 9:2; Matt 4:16).

are also given of the places where the souls of the righteous and the souls of sinners shall await "the great judgment" (1 *Enoch* 22).

ORAL PERFORMANCE FEATURES: SOUND, RHYTHM, EMOTION, AND METAPHORS

The woe oracle begins with the term *ouai*—an onomatopoetic interjection that imitates someone screaming in pain.[143] It is more of a sound than a word—a sound that functions to gain the audience's attention and to audibly communicate the pain that the false teachers are to experience because of their transgressions. The main purpose of sound imitation is to enhance the imagery of the scene, thereby giving substance to bare words. Aaron Schart imagines the sound of *ouai* as a "long, protracted scream in a high pitch that slowly subsides and eventually changes to sobbing."[144] The greater the pain, the louder the scream. Consequently, a translation that better captures the term as an emotional cry of pain is "Oh no!" or "Oh ah!"

In Jude's oracle, the scream represents an expression of the pain to be experienced by the false teachers upon the execution of their judgment. With the proper volume and pitch, the dark timber and intensity of this word could have been adequately expressed by the lector reading Jude's oracle. Aristotle pointed out that delivery is a matter of how the voice should be used in expressing each emotion, sometimes loud and sometimes soft and sometimes intermediate (*Rhetoric* 1403b26–31).

Following the woe oracle, several other sound features contribute to the emotional tone of verses 12 and 13, which describe the destructiveness and future condemnation of the false teachers.[145] One element in speech that can exploited for emotional affect is rhythm.[146] Rhythm transpires when there is the periodic

---

143. Mourning was loud and expressive (cf. Amos 5:16).

144. Schart, "Deathly Silence," n.p.

145. These features are noted by Alexandra Robinson (*Jude on the Attack*, 188–89).

146. Stanford, *Greek Tragedy*, 63.

reemergence of the same significant element or factor. The repeating sound features include, first, five neuter nominatives in verse 12 (trees, autumn, without fruit, dead, uprooted), all ending with the same vowel sound "ah," which adds beat to the phrase describing the character of the false teachers (*dendra, phthinopōrina, akarpa, apothanonta, ekrizōthenta*). Second, the three negative terms (without fear, waterless, fruitless) are all alliterated (*aphobōs, anydroi, akarpa*). Finally, in verse 13, the description of the destination of the wandering stars are depicted using a series of single and double syllable words ("for whom the deepest darkness," *hois, ho, zophos, tou, skotous, eis*), which speeds up the rhythm of the sentence.

Emotional intensity is also created by employing six consecutive metaphors highlighting the false teacher's destructiveness. Metaphors are particularly effective in an oral setting because its imagery most often appeals to the eye (Cicero, *De oratore* 3.160–165). According to Pseudo-Longinus, this is called using "visualizations" (*phantasiai*) and it describes passages where the writer has been inspired by strong emotion to the point that he visualizes what he wishes to describe and then brings it vividly before the eyes of the audience (*De sublimitate* 15). These verbal images give a new experience to Jude's listeners, helping them to see more clearly the realities of the false teachers. Describing the teachers as nature in chaos not only pinpoints their destructiveness but also alerts the listeners that the presence of the false teachers are signs that the last days are upon them. It gives a sense of urgency to their situation and serves as a warning to be prepared for the imminent return of Jesus.

Further, metaphors can encourage audience participation. By not stating something explicitly the audience is invited to unpack the nature of the association between the metaphor and referent. Quintilian underlines the rhetorical value of hinting at arguments instead of stating everything explicitly (*Institutio oratoria* 9.2.71–76). Audiences will be encouraged to participate by seeking out the comparison in the metaphor, which they would not believe

67

if they heard it openly stated but are more likely to believe if they discover it themselves.

The emotive description of the destiny of the false teachers to a place of eternal deep darkness was meant to invoke fear in a listening audience (v. 13). Hans Dieter Betz has demonstrated how journeys to the afterworld were used by Greek philosophers from Plato to Plutarch to induce a sense of fear and to give emotional power to their writing.[147] One example of this strategy describes an individual who undergoes a sudden conversion after a journey of his soul to the afterlife where he sees the punishments for sins of many of his acquaintances, including his father (Plutarch, *De sera numinis vindicta* 22–24).[148] It was likely Jude's intent was also to warn his listeners about avoiding the fate of the intruders or attempting to bring about a conversion of others in the congregation.

APPLICATION OF THE TEXT

With the persistent emphasis on divine judgment, coupled with Jude's emotional and invective language, perhaps one can understand how individuals can sometimes perceive of God as "angry" in the sense of being violent and hostile, making judgment an act of "wrath." From the strictly human point of view, "wrath" implies strong, stern, or fierce anger—it carries the emotional impact of deeply resentful indignation and ire that crushingly strikes out and destroys.[149] However, this is not to see God correctly. The intention of God in bringing to bear judgment upon humanity is not death but life, not obliteration but restoration, not disintegration but reconciliation (cf. Jonah 3:4; 4:1–2; Hos 2:14–15).[150] The purpose of judgment is grace, the healing of the hurt and disruption of dis-grace. It is fulfilling the inner purposes of God—that all things become what they truly are created to become and thereby

---

147. Betz, "Problem of Apocalyptic Genre," 577–97.
148. See also Plato, *Gorgias* 523–25.
149. Ashbrook, "Judgment," 2.
150. Ashbrook, "Judgment," 2.

are transparent to his presence and show forth his glory.¹⁵¹ Given that judgment was still future for the ungodly in Jude, it was only a warning, and thus, transformation and reconciliation with God was (and is) still possible for those on the wrong path. We will learn more about transformation and reconciliation later in Jude.

Through metaphors of nature in disarray, Jude conveys that the presence of the intruders is a sign of the moral and natural decline that will transpire as the consummation of history nears. The signs of the end are a frequent topic among some Christians, often involving so much focus that it becomes obsessive and distracting. While the possibility that Christ's return may happen at any time, we must plan that it could be still distant. It should not take us by surprise. Not because we can predict it, but that we are always ready for and expecting it.¹⁵² Language of Christ's imminent return is a call for readiness, for righteous living, so that whenever the end occurs—cosmically or for us individually—we will be prepared to enter a new existence with God. To be ready means to stay in God's love, having faith in him, fearing him, and repenting before him. Readiness also means not being idle but instead putting our resources and spiritual gifts to work for the advancement of the kingdom. Agents of the kingdom are to make a significant difference in the world. Finally, to be ready means to avoid the vices and behaviors that Christ deplores and engage in the behaviors and spiritual disciplines he exhorts (cf. Rev 2–3).¹⁵³

TEXT: JUDE 14-16

> 14 It was also about these that Enoch, in the seventh generation from Adam, prophesied, saying, "See, the Lord is coming¹⁵⁴ with ten thousands of his holy ones, 15 to

---

151. Ashbrook, "Judgment," 2.
152. Lewis and Demarest, *Integrative Theology*, 3.435.
153. Lewis and Demarest, *Integrative Theology*, 3.439.
154. In Greek, the verb is in the past tense (came). However, Jude views the passage as predictive and the NRSV translates it accordingly ("is coming").

execute judgment on all, and to convict everyone[155] of all the deeds of ungodliness that they have committed in such an ungodly way, and of all the harsh things that ungodly sinners have spoken against him." 16 These are grumblers and malcontents; they indulge their own lusts;[156] they are bombastic in speech, flattering people to their own advantage.

EXPLANATION OF THE TEXT: A PROPHECY FROM ENOCH

Jude continues to refer to the interlopers by the pronoun "these," effectively setting boundaries between the godly and ungodly. To support his argument concerning the end of "these," Jude cites the extra-biblical Jewish text of *1 Enoch* (vv. 14–15). Jude must have understood that the prophetic text was authoritative. Indeed, as a prophecy it has a divine origin. Jude's citation is from the prophet Enoch who walked with God (Gen 5:24)[157] and was the seventh antediluvian patriarch, son of Jared and father of Methuselah (Gen 5:3–21; 1 Chr 1:1–3).[158] According to Jewish tradition, Enoch was taken up to heaven and was given access to the heavenly realm, its activities, and revelations about the future (e.g., *1 Enoch* 41:1, 80:1;

---

155. Literally "and to convict *all souls*" (*kai elenxai pasan psychēn*). Some manuscripts have "and to convict *all the ungodly*" (*kai elenxai pantas tous asebeis*, so ESV).

156. Although *epithymia* frequently suggests an emphasis on sexual appetites and sexual misconduct, it need not always, and often does not, have a sexual meaning except in certain contexts. Jude's point here is not so much that they indulge sinful desires, but that they follow their own desires rather than God's.

157. The phrase translated "Enoch walked with God" (*'ĕlōhîm*) in Gen 5:22 can be interpreted either as a sign of his piety toward God or his association with angels. The Hebrew term *'ĕlōhîm* in Gen 5:22 can mean superhuman beings including God(s) and angels (BDB, "אלהים" [*'ĕlōhîm*], 43).

158. As the seventh in line from Adam, Enoch is marked as an "elect one," chosen by God for a special destiny. This is based on the significance of the number seven in the ancient world (Alexander, "From Son of Adam," in Stone and Bergren, *Biblical Figures Outside the Bible*, 91).

Jubilees 4:17). Living just before the flood, Enoch's piety would have set him apart from his wicked generation. This suggests for him a prophetic role, rebuking his contemporaries and warning them of impending judgment.[159] His judgment over the fallen Watchers, combined with the fact that he did not see death, led to the idea that Enoch would return at the end of history to take part in the great final judgment.[160]

The prophesies against godless people in *1 Enoch* were re-applied by Jude to his opponents. Four times the prophecy calls the intruders ungodly. "Ungodliness" is not merely a collection of actions or utterances, but a state of disobedience (cf. Rom 1:18).[161] The prophecy is a citation of *1 Enoch* 1:9, which Jude has slightly altered. One of the changes made was the replacement of the word "he" (which in its original context refers to God) with the phrase "the Lord" (likely meaning Jesus).

It is not clear if Jude intended the prophecy to convey that at Jesus's second advent, 1) he will carry out judgment on all humanity, or 2) he will execute a first act of judgment on all humanity and then a second act of convicting the ungodly, or 3) he will execute judgment and conviction exclusively on the ungodly. In view of Jude's negative focus on the ungodly, it is likely he intended that the prophecy to speak of the universal divine judgment on the impious and all their vices.

Jude criticizes his opponents for many sins (v. 16), but in these verses he levels his most emphatic condemnation for their sins of speech, which progresses from grumbling to faultfinding to patronizing.[162] Here Pheme Perkins is helpful. She says, "Speech is much more carefully controlled and monitored in a traditional, hierarchical society than it is in modern democracies."[163] It is hard to realize the sense of horror at sins of speech that ancient society felt because for us words do not have the same power that they

---

159. Alexander, "From Son of Adam," 91.
160. Alexander, "From Son of Adam," 91.
161. Kraftchick, *Jude & 2 Peter*, 58.
162. Bateman, *Jude*, 320.
163. Perkins, *First and Second Peter*, 273–74.

do in traditional cultures.[164] In modern societies, words appear to have considerably less consequences than actions compared to traditional societies, where the word is a form of action.[165]

ORAL AND PERFORMANCE FEATURES: QUOTATIONS, REPETITION, AND AUDIENCE ENGAGEMENT

Three oral and performance features stand out in Enoch's prophecy against the ungodly. First, is the introduction of Enoch and the quotation of his prophetic words. Second, is the repetition of a selection of sounds and words. Finally, the use of an audience attention prompter operates as an effective way to wake up the listeners and point to the importance of what is about to be recounted in the prophecy.

The mention of the prophet Enoch and the citation of his oracle in the performance of the letter means that the revered ancestor is in some sense invoked to be present amid the congregation.[166] The reperformance of Enoch's words served to render him in attendance, restating his warning of the forthcoming judgment of the ungodly. In doing so, the prophetic warning gains force and persuasiveness as if being heard for the first time spoken by the prophet himself. In the reading of Enoch's prophecy, the lector was not simply giving the impression of the character of Enoch, rather in performance the prophet reappears. A transformation occurs at the moment of performance. The lector is not himself and at the same time he is himself—coexisting as multiple personalities. The lector served an important role in helping Jude convey Enoch's words, directness, surety, and the portentous tone and ultimately his prophetic message to his listening audience.

The quoted prophecy is remarkable for its repetition. First, the stem *aseb-* is repeated four times (*asebeis* [twice], *asebeias*,

---

164. Perkins, *First and Second Peter*, 273–74.
165. Perkins, *First and Second Peter*, 273–74.
166. Loubser, "Invoking the Ancestors," 136.

ēsebēsan [ungodly]).¹⁶⁷ Second, the term "all" (*panton, pantas*) is also used four times. This overkill through repetition, whether spoken aloud or read silently, serves to dramatically proclaim the comprehensive nature of the false teacher's character, which is antithetical to all things related to God. When spoken, a lector could quite naturally intone these words more forcefully. Third, in addition to these repeated words, in four of the prophecy's clauses, sounds are repeated.¹⁶⁸ The repeated sounds (those that were likely intentional) and repeated words are marked in the translation below, demonstrating that clauses c and e have repeated sounds as do clauses d and f. A final pattern appears in clauses a and b where parallelism exhibits repeated thoughts (*poiēsai krisin* [to execute judgment] = *elenxai* [to convict]).¹⁶⁹ The numerous repetitions in verse 15 create a rhythm, giving the prophecy a marked poetic diction.

a *poiēsai krisin kata* **pantōn**

to execute judgment on all

b *kai elenxai* **pantas** *tous* **asebeis**

and to convict every ungodly person

c *peri* **pantōn** *tōn ergōn* **asebeias** *autōn*

of all their ungodly deeds

d *hōn* **ēsebēsan**

that they have committed in an ungodly manner

e *kai peri* **pantōn** *tōn sklērōn*

and all the harsh things

f *hōn elalēsan kat' autou hamartōloi* **asebeis**

which ungodly sinners have spoken against him.¹⁷⁰

---

167. Bauckham, *2 Peter, Jude*, 97.
168. Charles, "Literary Artifice," 114.
169. Charles, "Literary Artifice," 113.
170. My translation.

According to Jude 15, Enoch *proephēteusen* (prophesied), which by its very nature meant he delivered a divine message to a human audience (e.g., Jer 1:9; Isa 51:16). Texts like the prophecy from Enoch, which recount divine revelations, have generally been highly and even exceptionally poetic texts.[171] Poetry in the ancient world was considered the language of the gods. The oracles at Delphi, with the priestess of Apollo, as well as the sibyls at various sites in the ancient world like Cumae (near Naples), delivered their prophecies typically in hexameter verses.[172] The Muses gave poets the ability to craft beautiful songs and poems (e.g., Homer, *Odyssey* 8.478–481; Hesiod, *Theogony* 22).[173] In the Hellenistic and Roman periods, the Greeks widely accepted the divine inspiration of poetry (e.g., Homer, *Odyssey* 8.44–45, 62–64, 488, 498; 17.518; 22.347).[174] Socrates stated that poets "don't do what they do from wisdom, but from some natural inspiration, like prophets and oracle mongers" (Plato, *Apology of Socrates* 22b8–c2). Again, Socrates remarked about the poet, "For the god, as it seems to me, intended him to be a sign to us that we should not waver or doubt that these fine poems are not human or the work of men, but divine and the work of gods; and that the poets are merely the interpreters of the gods, according as each is possessed by one of the heavenly powers" (Plato, *Ion* 534e–535a).

The biblical prophets also composed their divine messages in a poetic and musical style (e.g., Isa 5; Ezek 33:32). Some of the Psalms, which are poetic by nature, contain oracles where God is addressing Israel, or the nations, or pagan deities (e.g., Pss 81:6–16; 82:2–7). As Robert Alter has said, poetry is our best human model of complex and rich communication, being "solemn, weighty, and forceful."[175] Enoch's poetic prophecy perhaps reinforced to Jude's

---

171. Heffelfinger, "More than Mere Ornamentation," 45.

172. Franke, "At the Creative Source of the Arts," n.p.

173. Murray, "Poetic Inspiration," 159.

174. Christopher Stanley argues that Homer was widely regarded as genuine divine truth in the first century Greco-Roman world ("Paul and Homer," 51–52).

175. Alter, *Art of Biblical Poetry*, 147.

audience that they were hearing more than human words but a divine declaration, thereby underscoring the prophecy's authority and trustworthiness.

Because of the danger associated with being in the divine presence (e.g., Gen 16:13; 32:30; Exod 33:18–20; Judg 6:22–23; 13:22), it might be argued that poetic language served as sort of a literary garb, clothing the divine voice in a "veil" to protect the listener from the searing vocal presence of God.[176] The aural presence of God was considered a threat to mortals (Exod 20:18–19; Deut 5:22–27). For example, when Elijah heard the voice of God, having been struck dumb, he wrapped his face in his mantle (1 Kgs 19:11–13). Consequently, it is appropriate that divine speech should be represented as poetry. By setting Enoch's prophecy in poetry, Jude was "putting divine speech in special divine speech quotation marks."[177]

The lector not only personified the human dimension when reading the letter aloud, but also the divine. In some ways when a lector read Enoch's prophecy to the original audience, he was inviting them into an encounter with the aural presence of God. While the divine word in the form of a poetic prophecy conferred a message, it was also a means of an experience and encounter with the divine speaker.[178] Poetry persuades, not through argument alone, but through encounter—encounter with the voice that speaks through the prophet.

Given that Enoch's prophecy was literally the voice of God, would the words have been vocalized any differently by the lector or reader? The gods do not talk like humans. Homeric gods and the God of Scripture sound different from mortals. They are greater than humans, and so it is only natural that their voices are louder. A god's shout sounds as loud as nine thousand or ten thousand warriors (Homer, *Iliad* 5.859–61, 14.147–51), sending mortals into panic (e.g., *Iliad* 5.862–3, 15.320 24; Homer, *Odyssey*

---

176. Geller, "Were the Prophets Poets?" 212.

177. Katie Heffelfinger makes this statement regarding the prophetic oracles of the Old Testament ("More than Mere Ornamentation," 38).

178. Heffelfinger, "More than Mere Ornamentation," 52.

24.48–9, 530–35).[179] God spoke to the Israelites on the mountain with a voice that caused them great fear (Exod 20:18–19; Deut 5:22–27). In the Old Testament, terror of people experiencing the divine audible presence may be attributed to the volume of his voice, as God's speech is often characterized as "mighty," "powerful," "roaring," or "thunderous" (e.g., 1 Sam 7:10; 2 Sam 22:14; Pss 29:4; 46:6; Job 37:2; Jer 25:30; Amos 1:2). In Revelation, the one like the son of man is described as having a loud voice, imitating both the sound of many waters (1:15) and a trumpet (1:10). The voice from heaven (14:2) and from the heavenly throne (21:3) also broadcast loudly like many waters.

Did the lector raise his voice to reflect that God was speaking or articulate in a tone to lend credence to the confidence reflected in the prophecy? There are inevitable limitations and a fair amount of speculation in attempting to determine the way a biblical passage was initially delivered. The original performances are lost, but it is important to note that in the ancient Mediterranean world, impersonation of a figure was a highly valued rhetorical device. Professional speakers employed impersonation to achieve a variety of purposes such as to display the inner thoughts of adversaries and to introduce conversations between themselves and others.[180] Impersonation or prosopopoiia is the act of giving voice to a figure such as an opponent, a fictive representative of a people, an ancient nobleman raised from the dead, or even to bring down the gods from heaven in order to strengthen the argument of the author or speaker who employs the device.[181] Pseudo-Longinus felt that by mimicking the style of past authorities it endowed a speaker with inspiration and expressiveness as if his words were an emanation from a holy tongue ([*De sublimitate*] 13.2–3). According to Quintilian, these impersonations can be used 1) to reveal an opponent's inner thoughts, 2) to introduce imaginary conversations, or 3) to supply an opportunity for the author to advise, to rebuke, to complain, to praise, or to mourn (Quintilian, *Institutio oratoria*

---

179. As noted by Heath, *Talking Greeks*, 52.
180. Ward and Trobisch, *Bringing the Word to Life*, 15.
181. Dodson, *"Powers" of Personification*, 36.

9.2.30–31).[182] The speaker would take the character's fortune, social rank, and achievement into account, then communicate these elements by means of suitable gestures and vocal intonations.[183] A skilled and prepared lector-reader, by utilizing an authoritative and confident tone, could present more fully that God was speaking when reciting Enoch's words.

Another performance feature present in the prophecy is the word *idou*, translated as "see" (v. 14). Nicholas Bailey has identified several functions of the Greek word *idou* in the New Testament.[184] One function Bailey identifies for the word, and it applies to its use here in Jude, is that it serves as a "prompter of attention" to instruct the hearer to pay special notice to something critical being said.[185] It is often translated as "look" or "see" because there is some similarity between a "metaphorical pointing" and those situations where physical pointing is used. If someone points out to you the physical presence of an entity or situation in the real world, he or she does so for some reason, for example, because that entity may be useful or harmful, interesting, or surprising. The same is true of a metaphorical pointing. Like in English, also in Greek and other languages, one can say "look!" when one does not expect the hearer to physically look but rather to pay attention to what is being said or about to be said.[186]

Rather than "see" or "look" a better translation for *idou* in Jude's quote of Enoch's prediction would be "take note!" or "think long and carefully about what I am going to say." Further, this version of the word *idou* also heralds strong and certain statements that count as promises and predictions, warnings, curses, and judgments,[187] which suits Jude's purpose here to emphasize the certain future condemnation of the ungodly. The boldness of the term helps Jude encourage his listeners to share his perspective

---

182. As noted by Dodson, *"Powers" of Personification*, 36, 37.
183. Ward and Trobisch, *Bringing the Word*, 15.
184. Jude changes the word *hoti* in 1 Enoch 1:9 to *idou* (v. 14).
185. Bailey, "Thetic Constructions in Koine Greek," 361.
186. Bailey, "Thetic Constructions in Koine Greek," 362–63.
187. Bailey, "Thetic Constructions in Koine Greek," 376.

on these individuals. In addition to using these better translations and to accomplish all that the word *idou* intends for Jude, a lector might physically point to the letter before commencing his reading of Enoch's prophecy.

Finally, it is noteworthy that "grumblers," is the onomatopoetic word, *gongystai*, expressing the sound of a person muttering (v. 16). It is a sound-related device that must be heard for its full effect. Like most people who live only for themselves, the false teachers are unhappy, evidenced by their grumbling and complaining about circumstances that disappoint them (v. 16).[188] Jude may have intentionally used the same word, which the Septuagint employs to describe Israel in the wilderness who were also "grumblers" (*gongystai*) that complained against the Lord (e.g., Exod 16:7–9, 12; 17:3; Num 11:1).

Catrin Williams labels the act of recalling a past event like the grumbling Israelites in the wilderness and connecting it to a current event as "keying."[189] Keying interprets present realities by analogy. The association between two events is established in such a way that the temporal difference between the grumblers in the wilderness and the grumbling false teachers are collapsed to strengthen the connection between them. The behavior of the Israelites in the wilderness helps to explain God's reaction to the grumbling false teachers in the present. The Psalmist's sermon (Ps 78:18–22) about the event in the wilderness portrays God as incensed at the disbelief and faithlessness inherent in the people's grumbling—a portrayal Jude hoped to have his listeners see as God's perception of the false teachers' grumbling as well.

APPLICATION OF THE TEXT

Because of Jude's excessive and harsh criticism of the ungodly intruders, along with his emphasis on their future condemnation, it is tempting to hold a self-assured satisfaction that we are not

---

188. Schreiner, 1, 2 *Peter, Jude*, 415.
189. Williams, "How Scripture 'Speaks,'" 68.

among those to be judged. However, a word from God to us in these passages cannot be discarded too easily. Since the beginning of the letter, Jude has compiled quite a comprehensive list of the vices of the ungodly. They abuse divine grace and divine authority (vv. 4, 8). They are guilty of rebellion and slander (v. 8) which is to speak ill of someone (v. 10). They have committed sexual sins (v. 8), engaged in harsh speech against Christ (him),[190] and they are grumblers, malcontents (criticize), bombastic (haughty, pompous) in their speech, and flatter people for their own advantage (v. 15). While the impious intruders are specifically attached to these sins, Christians also commit these iniquities and thus, the emphasis on them in the letter also serves as a warning to everyone in the community. Though saved from the ultimate divine judgment, we need to guard against self-righteous gloating and remember that we have a responsibility for taking our shortcomings seriously. We still err and those sins need to be recognized and addressed.

One set of sins that seems to dominate Jude in this section are those related to speech. To point out these sins, as noted, Jude uses the onomatopoetic word *gongystai* for "grumblers." Complaining, criticizing, slandering, boasting, and flattery suggests that the ungodly in Jude's community talk too much. Too much talking undermines community life (cf. Col 3:8; Eph 4:31; 5:4). Words have power, both destructive (e.g., Prov 18:20-2; cf. Jas 3:9-10) and beneficial (cf. Jas 3:9-10). Because it is more difficult to avoid errors in speech than in any other aspect of daily life (cf. Jas 3:2), this section encourages us to be conscious of our depravity in this arena. One very basic reason why humans talk about anything is from a need to manipulate or control their environment, which includes other people. It is no wonder that the Bible has direct and stern words about speech. It consistently warns that God intervenes to uproot and destroy foolish speech and to judge those who speak in this way (e.g., Prov 10:14; 13:3; Matt 12:36-37).

---

190. The false teachers dispute the authority of God (or Christ). Instead of accepting his will for them, they resist it and complain about it (Bauckham, *Jude*, 99).

TEXT: JUDE 17-23

17 But you, beloved, must remember the predictions of the apostles of our Lord Jesus Christ; 18 for they said to you, "In the last time there will be scoffers,[191] indulging their own ungodly lusts." 19 It is these worldly people, devoid of the Spirit,[192] who are causing divisions. 20 But you, beloved, build yourselves[193] up on your most holy faith; pray in the Holy Spirit; 21 keep yourselves in the love of God; look forward to the mercy of our Lord Jesus Christ that leads to eternal life.[194] 22 And have mercy on some who are wavering;[195] 23 save others by snatching

---

191. In the Old Testament, the "scoffer" is one who shows disdain for wisdom and morality (e.g., Prov 1:22, 14:6; Ps 74:22). In the Qumran texts it was used for its enemy the wicked priest and his allies (e.g., Cairo Genizah copy of the *Damascus Document* 1:14)

192. *Pneuma* (Spirit) is without the definite article in Greek, which has led some to translate this as "they do not have a spirit." The use of *pneuma* without the article for the Holy Spirit is common in the New Testament (cf. John 3:5; 7:39; Gal 5:16 [Blum, "Jude," n.p.]).

193. The NLT indicates more clearly than the NRSV that the pronouns in verses 21 and 22 convey mutual care: "But you, dear friends, must build each other up in your most holy faith, pray in the power of the Holy Spirit, 21 and await the mercy of our Lord Jesus Christ, who will bring you eternal life. In this way, you will keep yourselves safe in God's love." The pronoun translated as "each other" is reciprocal, so that the work of building up is a community task in which all participate. It is not a job solely for church leadership but rather for the whole church. The command is not for each person to look after himself or herself, instead the command is for everyone to look out for each other in the church (Reese, *2 Peter and Jude*, 69).

194. Most translations have the participles in verses 20 and 21 function as imperatives (so, NRSV). However, three of the verbs are participles ("building," "praying," "looking forward") while the fourth is an imperative ("keep"). A better option is to treat the participles as the *means* by which the readers are to keep themselves in the love of God as in the following translation. "But you, dear friends, by building yourselves up in your most holy faith and praying in the Holy Spirit, *keep* yourselves in God's love as you wait for the mercy of our Lord Jesus Christ to bring you to eternal life" (NIV).

195. The verb translated here as "wavering" (*diakrinesthai*) has already appeared in verse 9 with the meaning "be at odds with," "dispute." Here it likely has the alternative meaning of doubt or waver.

them out of the fire; and have mercy on still others with fear, hating even the tunic defiled by their bodies.[196]

EXPLANATION OF THE TEXT: RESPONSIBILITY OF THE CHURCH

In verses 17–19 Jude's tone changes and his focus shifts. While the intruders remain a concern (v. 18), the needs of the letter recipients are the focus from here through the end of the letter.[197] Jude initially reminds the listeners of a prophesy from the apostles (vv. 17–18). As a forecast by Jesus's ambassadors, the words have both apostolic and divine authority. Jude does not quote any known apostolic text. He may be giving a verbatim quotation of some current apostolic formulation, or simply reflecting the essence of the many end-time warnings against false teachers given by the apostles (e.g., Matt 7:15; 24:11; Mark 13:22; Acts 20:29–30; 2 Pet 3:3). Nevertheless, the presence of the intruders should not surprise the letter recipients, because the apostles had already foretold of their appearance.

In typical threefold fashion Jude characterizes the ungodly—they are divisive, worldly, and devoid of the Spirit (v. 19). The gift

---

196. The manuscripts and versions containing verses 22 and 23 have various readings. However, they can be divided into two main groups: a shorter text consisting of two clauses and a longer text consisting of three clauses. An example of the two-clause translation is as follows: "And on some have compassion, making a distinction; but others save with fear, pulling them out of the fire, hating even the garment defiled by the flesh" (NKJV). A case for the originality of the shortest reading can be made based on its attestation, its suitability to the context in Jude, and because it is possible to explain the various longer readings as expansions and adaptations of it (Bauckham, *Jude*, 110.) Most translations opt for the three-clause version, which can be supported by Jude's penchant for groups of three. Jude's text can also be read as referring to one group: "Have mercy on those who are doubting; save them, seizing them from the fire; have mercy on them with fear, hating even the garment stained by the flesh." As noted by Michaels, "Finding Yourself an Intercessor," 249.

197. Kraftchick, *Jude & 2 Peter*, 58.

of God's Spirit establishes someone as a member of God's elect community (2 Cor 1:22; Eph 1:13–14; Gal 4:6; 5:25).[198]

Next Jude exhorts his audience to practice four behaviors in their Christian life (vv. 20–21). These ritual activities are focused on the maintenance of boundaries to determine who is part of the church and who is not.[199] To help them remember the instructions, Jude uses two triadic formulas that form part of the basis of the Christian belief: "faith, love, and hope" and "God, Christ, and the Holy Spirit." The believers are to build each other up on the holy faith, which here refers to the gospel. It is holy because it comes from God. Second, they are to pray in the control of the Spirit or under the inspiration of the Spirit (cf. Rom 8:26–27). Praying in the Spirit includes, but is not limited to, prayer in tongues (1 Cor 14:15–16).[200] Finally, they should also keep each other in God's love (cf. John 15:9), while waiting for the mercy of Christ to inaugurate the eschatological hope of eternal life.

Jude then commands his audience to undertake three actions toward others in their midst who are in peril (vv. 22–23). First, they are to extend mercy to those within the church who waver or are doubting (v. 22a). Perhaps the teaching and example of the false teachers have caused them to be uncertain about the truth of Christianity. The second group needs to be dealt with directly and vigorously, snatching them out of the fire of damnation. Toward the final group, Christians are to show mercy, while also exercising caution, being fearful of contamination by the sinful practices of these individuals. This group of people appears to be deep in the immorality of the false teachers or perhaps are the false teachers themselves. Jude may be interested not only in preserving the spiritual health of the church but also in reclaiming the intruders from their error.[201] Further, it is noteworthy that in the letter Jude does not require that the intruders be expelled from the church.[202]

---

198. Kraftchick, *Jude & 2 Peter*, 62.
199. Joubert, "Language, Ideology," 346.
200. Bauckham, *2 Peter, Jude*, 113.
201. Painter and deSilva, *James and Jude*, 224.
202. Painter and deSilva, *James and Jude*, 224.

Commentary on Jude

ORAL AND PERFORMANCE FEATURES: IRONY, ALLUSION, RHETORICAL STYLE, AND EMOTIONS

Ancient storytellers and orators used subtleties in their speech to express and emphasize their points of view in a variety of ways, including through irony (*eirōneia*).[203] One reason speakers used irony was that it was more emphatic than making a point-blank statement of the truth. It causes the listener, who does not have the text in front of them, to pause and contemplate a point the author desires to communicate. Often it underscores a particular theology. Another purpose in using irony is that the listener is more likely to remember the point when it is expressed in ironic form. The listener should take time and reflect on these unexpected twists present in the text. Ironically, the scoffers, who are a threat to the church, serve as aids to the congregation's faith because the fulfilled prediction shows God's sovereign foreknowledge—he was fully aware of the scoffers' eventual appearance in the church.[204]

The instructions regarding how the church was to deal with those under the influence of the ungodly contains a couple of echoes to Zechariah 3:1–5. Zechariah 3 recounts an episode set in the heavenly courtroom where Satan accuses Joshua the high priest in the presence of the angel of the Lord. Silencing the accusation, the Lord rebukes Satan and restores Joshua, proclaiming over him: "Is not this man a brand plucked from the fire?" (3:2b). This reference in Jude and the phrase a "tunic defiled by their bodies" (v. 23) also echoes Zechariah's description of Joshua's "filthy" clothes (Zech 3:3).

In its original context, the phrase "plucked from fire" represents Joshua's release from exile in Babylon. The fire was an image for exile, which placed Joshua in a defiled state, and thus made him unfit for a priestly role. A defiled state was also unsuitable for a person in the presence of God. However, God's declaration has

---

203. "Irony is the use of words which in the context convey a contrary meaning" (Porter, *Handbook of Classical Rhetoric*, 128). Quintilian stated that ironic statements are are to be understood in a sense other than what is stated plainly (*Institutio oratoria* 6.2.16).

204. Kraftchick, *Jude & 2 Peter*, 59.

restored Joshua, removing his unclean garments, and fitting him in clean clothes.

Jude was counting on his audiences' knowledge of this narrative to solicit their mental involvement and gain their attention. Further, the allusion to this narrative would help Jude to communicate what he expects of his listeners regarding treating those in peril.

With Zechariah providing the backdrop to Jude's instruction, even the opponents, though defiled and facing righteous judgment, are offered the hope of restoration.[205] In the context of Jude, those on the verge of following the false teachers into sin, even those that have already fallen into sin, are to be plucked from their perilous situation. Mercy is to be extended to the needy to reflect the goodness of God, but without tolerance for the instructions of the ungodly teachers.[206]

In addition to these allusions from Zechariah, in the same verses, Jude also makes effective use of epanaphora where the same word(s) *kai hous . . . hous de . . . hous de* ("on some . . . on others . . . on others"; vv. 22–23) begin successive phrases.[207] The following translation captures the effect of the device.

> And on some who doubt, have mercy;
> on some, save, by snatching them out of the fire;
> on some have mercy with fear, hating even the garment
>   polluted by the flesh.[208]

One of the reasons for the piling up of subordinate clauses that are introduced by the same words is that here the repetition gives Jude's instructions a sense of rhythm. The rhythmic aesthetics of Jude's words might have mesmerized listeners, making a listener more receptive to the content. Vessela Valiavitcharska

---

205. Lockett, "Objects of Mercy in Jude," 334–36.
206. Lockett, "Objects of Mercy in Jude," 334–36.
207. *Rhetorica ad Herennium* 4.13.19; Demetrius, *De elocutione* 268; Cicero, *De oratore* 3.54.206; Quintilian, *Institutio oratoria* 9.3.30.
208. My translation.

remarks that rhythm has significant power.[209] If surrendered to, rhythm commands the human psyche and carries away judgment, making it the ultimate rhetorical tool.[210]

Finally, fear is elicited in this section both directly and indirectly. Emotive language can be direct or indirect. Direct emotional language is indicated when emotional words (e.g., hope, fear, jealousy, anger) are specifically mentioned in the text. An example of language carrying indirect but no less forcible emotive feelings is the sentence "the boy fell asleep and never woke up again." The unpleasant emotion is not explicitly stated, but the sentence triggers negative, depressed feelings—because the emotion is implied. Thus, in addition to the direct mention of emotions, context can indicate a passionate situation. The emotion of fear is awakened indirectly because Christians under the influence of the false teachers are in danger of punishment by fire. And fear is also provoked directly as Jude warns his audience that their approach to those in peril should be done so in "fear." Those in peril constitute a danger to Jude's listeners. They face the possibility of being contaminated by the sinner's sin in trying to rescue their brothers and sisters. If contaminated, they too will face the judgment of God. So here the fear likely represents a reverence and respect for God and his hatred of sin and judgment of sinners.[211] In emotive warnings like this, orators are instructed to use a deep-toned voice (Quintilian, *Institutio oratoria* 11.3.64), and a slower speed of delivery to emphasize it (Quintilian, *Institutio oratoria* 11.3.112). A well-prepared lector would enhance Jude's warning if intoned in this manner.

Imploring his listeners to "save others by snatching them out of the fire" (v. 23) is emotive and apocalyptic language, implying that some in the church are so far into sin that they are currently experiencing the flames of the end time judgment.[212] To the extent

---

209. Valiavitcharska, *Rhetoric and Rhythm*, 1.

210. Valiavitcharska, *Rhetoric and Rhythm*, 1.

211. Kelly, *Epistles of Peter and of Jude*, 289.

212. Harm W. Hollander argues that "fire" is a metaphor for the false teachers and their wicked ideas rather than the fires of hell ("Attitude towards

that it succeeds in convincing its audience, apocalyptic language cannot avoid enacting the end it references by vividly evoking the terror to transpire for some at the consummation of history.[213] Thus, successfully evoking experiences of the imminent end is to bring the end closer by performing it rhetorically, while also creating a sense of urgency to the situation of the lost, who are in grave peril and need immediate rescuing.

APPLICATION OF THE TEXT

While the scoffers were detrimental to the redeemed community, ironically the prediction of their appearance served to strengthen the faith of the church by reminding them of God's sovereignty. It is encouraging to know that there are no unexpected events in the plans of God. Jude's stress on divine foreknowledge and authoritative rule is an important meditation for all Christians—both those experiencing life's turmoil and those momentarily free from its affects. Everything that happens in human history is known by God and it happens just as he knows it will. God is the Lord and determiner of history. Knowledge of the future, such as that expressed in God's awareness of the scoffers' arrival conveys the notion of divine foreknowledge. Everything unfolds according to a divine plan. God's people should not despair. All things happen in a time fixed by God. We do not have to spend our life worrying because God is in charge. We need to remember his sovereignty when we

---

Christians," 123–34). He bases this claim on the fact that the verb in the Greek translated as "snatch" is used in other contexts to indicate saving or protecting somebody from a present danger rather than from a future danger ("Attitude towards Christians," 127). However, the word is also used in certain contexts to communicate a violent act on a subject (e.g., Judg 21:21 LXX). Jude clearly is not intending a violent act but a rescue. Word use in other contexts is not sufficient proof to conclude that Jude is not referencing an act to prevent someone from a future punishment in hell. Further, considering Jude's fondness for contrasts (see Charles, "Polemic and Persuasion," 913–14), the fire (of hell) contrasts nicely with the redeemed standing in the presence of God's glory (v. 24).

213. O'Leary, "Dramatistic," 412–13.

are faced with impossible situations. "It is an amazing thing that God can rule all of history on the broadest level and at the same time, micromanage every instant of every individual life without losing control or making mistakes."[214]

Jude's instruction for rescuing sinners, set in a sing-song style together with the use of emotional language conveys a sense of importance. Jude's methodology helps to communicate the need for a swift, direct, and vigorous approach to reaching the lost. For Jude, today is the day of salvation, procrastination is not an option. We should embrace this urgency and direct involvement in the task of harvesting crops of souls that will be able to enjoy the great eschatological banquet rather than be subject to the alternative end they would face. We must be ready to speak in a timely fashion rather than only live by example. Sometimes we hesitate to speak, but there are many times when silence is cowardly and can cause more harm than speaking out could ever cause.[215] There are those who must be snatched from the fire. They have started out on the wrong path and must be stopped.

The emphasis in these instructions also reminds the church of divine grace, unmerited and yet available through God's faithfulness. Jude combines abhorrence for the sins the false teachers are promoting and a strong belief in God's judgment on sin with a genuinely Christian concern for the reclamation of even the most obstinate.[216]

TEXT: JUDE 24-25

24 Now[217] to him who is able to keep you from falling, and to make you stand[218] without blemish in the

214. Crawford, unpublished "Notes for Systematic Theology I," 527.
215. Barclay, *Letters of John and Jude*, 234.
216. Bauckham, *2 Peter, Jude*, 117–18.
217. As discussed previously, note the adverb "now" (*de*), which may have served to indicate a change in volume or tone in the doxology.
218. The term translated as "stand" refers to eschatological vindication at God's throne on the last day (1 Cor 10:12; cf. Eph 6:11, 13, 14).

presence of his glory with rejoicing, 25 to the only God our Savior, through Jesus Christ our Lord, be glory, majesty, power, and authority, before all time and now and forever. Amen.

EXPLANATION OF THE TEXT: CLOSING DOXOLOGY

Jude finishes his letter with a doxology, which is also a form of praise or prayer. It includes an ascription to God emphasizing that he alone can save and preserve the worshipper from ruin at the judgment, presenting them without blemish so he or she may rejoice in the divine presence. "Without blemish" originally had tabernacle and temple associations, denoting that the sacrificial animal was free from blemish—a quality that God required (e.g., Exod 29:1; Lev 1:3; 10). It is used here to signify the integrity and moral purity of the redeemed (Ps 15:2; Prov 11:5; Eph 1:4; 5:27; Heb 9:14).[219]

The doxology also ascribes glory, majesty, power, and authority to God. This does not signify that the worshipper is adding something to God that is currently not a part of his nature, but instead it acknowledges his existing divine perfections.[220] Power and authority are straightforward. However, "glory" and "majesty" deserve comment. Given that God accomplishes the keeping and saving of people, he deserves to be ascribed the "glory" or public honor, acclamation, and praise.[221] "Majesty" denotes his greatness or "His awful transcendence."[222] In a solemn-sounding phrase God is declared to possess these perfections from all eternity: before all time, now, and forever.[223] Like the typical doxology, it concludes with an invitation for the hearers to affirm the honors offered to

---

219. Kelly, *Epistles of Peter and of Jude*, 290–94.
220. Weima, *Neglected Endings*, 138.
221. Neyrey, *2 Peter, Jude*, 97.
222. Kelly, *Epistles of Peter and of Jude*, 293.
223. Kelly, *Epistles of Peter and of Jude*, 290–94.

God, to which the "amen" was the congregation's confirmatory response (cf. 1 Chr 16:36; Ps 106:48; cf. also 1 Cor 14:16).

ORAL AND PERFORMANCE FEATURES: SOUND, EMOTIONS, AUDIENCE PARTICIPATION, AND REPETITION

As Bo Reicke stated, this doxology is "grand and soul stirring."[224] In addition to the grandeur of the words, the sound of the praise when spoken in Greek would have enhanced its robust character. The reverent doxology draws in the audience emotionally and verbally.

One way that sounds are thought to have the capacity to contribute to the robust nature of a text is related to the position of the tongue and jaw when different vowels are enunciated. The acoustics produced by the various vowel sounds are generally categorized relative to the position of the tongue and the jaw during pronunciation.[225] For the vowel vocalization of a long *i* as in *light*, the front of the tongue is high in the mouth and the jaw more closed.[226] For the vowel sound of a short *a* as in *ladder*, the tongue and jaw are lowered.[227] If a physician were to ask his patients to say "*i*" he would be not able to check his or her throat.[228] He or she needs a wide open mouth and flat tongue such as when one pronounces the word "pot." Research has demonstrated that as the tongue moves from the top to the bottom of the mouth and as the mouth is more open (jaw lowered) in the pronunciation of different vowels, a person's perception of size increases.[229] The various positions of the jaw and tongue and the resulting sound creates a

---

224. Reicke, *Epistles of James*, 217.

225. Shrum and Lowrey, "Sounds Convey Meaning," 41; Devine and Stephens, *The Prosody of Greek Speech*, 16; French, "Toward an Explanation of Phonetic Symbolism," 305–22; Jakobson and Waugh, *Sound Shape*, 181–90.

226. Devine and Stevens, *Prosody of Greek Speech*, 16.

227. Devine and Stevens, *Prosody of Greek Speech*, 16.

228. Devine and Stevens, *Prosody of Greek Speech*, 16.

229. Shrum and Lowrey, "Sounds Convey Meaning," 41.

sound-meaning relationship. For example, in a study of two nonsense words, *mil* and *mal* participants were asked to associate the terms with either a large table or small one. The majority associated *mil* with a small table and *mal* with a large table.[230] In *mil* the tongue is lower, and the mouth is more closed (small) compared to the vocalization of *mal* (large). The point is that certain vowels sound bigger or louder than others.[231] In pronouncing the syllable *cha–* the mouth is opened to a full extent "in order to sound the aspiration of the palatal in front of the following open vowel."[232] Consequently, many of the Greek terms meaning yawn, gale, and guffaw begin with that syllable.[233] Of all the Greek vowels, those that are associated with increased volume and size (the lowest jaw position when pronounced) are *e, a* (long and short forms), and *o*.

The ancient theorists were aware of the connection between the sound of certain vowels and their potential to contribute to meaning. Dionysius, in his grammar handbook, discussed the sound-meaning association based on jaw positions. He stated, "The short vowels, or those which are pronounced short, are inferior, because they lack volume and restrict sound. Again, of the long vowels, the one with the best sound is *a*, when lengthened, for it is pronounced with the mouth open to the fullest extent and the breath forced upwards to the palate."[234] He went on to say, "Of the short vowels neither is beautiful, but *o* is less ugly than *e*: for the former causes the mouth to open wider than the latter, and receives the impact more in the region of the windpipe."[235] He felt the long vowels *a, ē, ō,* and *y* were the "most powerful."[236]

230. Shrum and Lowrey, "Sounds Convey Meaning," 41.
231. Jakobson and Waugh, *Sound Shape*, 185.
232. Stanford, *Sound of Greek*, 185.
233. Stanford, *Sound of Greek*, 104, 185.
234. Dionysius, *De compositione verborum* 14, 97.
235. Dionysius, *De compositione verborum* 14, 97.
236. Dionysius, *De compositione verborum* 14. John B. Foley makes similar arguments to those of Dionysius. Foley makes a distinction between complex (long *A, E, U*) and pure vowels (those which when spoken include no motion of the mouth, tongue or lips such as *I* ("Aural Basis for Oral Liturgical Prayer," 132–52). Complex vowels sound bigger or louder than others. Complex vowels

Authors like Jude, knowing their compositions were to be recited aloud, were aware the sound of some vowels had the capacity to give the impression of increased size or volume. In comparison to the rest of the letter, the doxology in Jude contains a relatively large proportion of open mouth and powerful vowels. The use of various long vowels within words of the doxology help create the effect of size or grandeur in praise of God. The way it was originally vocalized would have reflected more fully the divine realities acknowledged in the address to God.

In addition to the open mouth vowels, the doxology contains a copious list of divine deeds and qualities—a literary technique known as amplification, which ancients employed to invest a subject one is speaking or writing about with grandeur (Longinus, *De sublimitate* 12.1).[237] As Cicero asserts, employing amplification could have the effect of arousing emotion (Cicero, *Partitiones oratoriae* 15.53).

Reverence and awe for God may have been stimulated in the hearing of Jude's doxology. Jonathan Haidt contends that awe is usually triggered when two situations are present: first, vastness (something larger than us overwhelms us and makes us feel small) and second, one's experience is not easily assimilated into existing mental structures.[238] Something that is vast or enormous, such as the distinctive attributes of God, cannot be mentally processed. When people are mystified, they feel small, powerless, and passive. When a person is confronted with a powerful social entity such as a deity, a response of awe and admiration can solidify social hierarchies, which are important for human survival.[239] Awe as-

---

have more energy and require more motion of the mouth, tongue, or lips to pronounce. They require more force or muscular energy, which translates into more energy when a sentence has a high volume of words with complex vowels. As the higher energy vowels increase in words and sentences, a particular statement will convey increased energy.

237. To assert a god's prominence, Greek prayers also contained heaped up epithets and excessive descriptions of the god's power (Pulleyn, *Prayer in Greek Religion*, 52).

238. Haidt, *Righteous Mind*, 228.

239. Keltner and Haidt, "Approaching Awe," 306.

sociated with the experience of being in the presence of an entity greater than the self, such as God, endows the being with higher-status, respect, and authority. A potential response of Jude's listeners might have involved heightened attention to Jude's words and ultimately to God. By endowing status to God, awe can motivate commitment to him, including setting aside one's own interests and goals in deference to the divine interests.

It is possible that the closing doxology was sung or spoken antiphonally in Jude's church or other early Christian church settings.[240] Verses 24 and 25 have a literary balance and cadence that suggests this type of use. For example, the two main Greek verbs translated as "to keep" and "make you stand" contain two qualifiers (blemish and rejoicing); the two names with appositions (God our savior and Jesus Christ our Lord), the four attributes (glory, majesty, power, authority), and the three-fold reference to past time, present, and future.[241] This arrangement is fitting for a call from a lector and a response by the audience.

Antiphonal singing was prominent in ancient Greek drama (e.g., Aeschylus and Sophocles). There is evidence in the Old Testament that antiphonal singing was practiced in temple worship (2 Chr 5:12–13; Neh 12:31–39). Jude's audience would have been familiar with antiphonal and responsive liturgy described in the texts of their sacred Scriptures (e.g., Exod 15:20–21; 1 Sam 18:7; 21:11; Ezra 3:11) and would have likely practiced it in their church gatherings.

Finally, the key word *tēreō* (keep), and *phy̆lassō* (keep, guard) which is repeated throughout the epistle, appears for the last time in the doxology. The recurrence of the word stresses the divine presence for both judgment and blessing. The faithful are kept safe for Jesus (v. 1). Rebellious angels are kept in eternal chains (v. 6). The deepest darkness has been kept (reserved) for the false teachers (v. 13), and finally God keeps the faithful from falling so they can stand in the divine presence (v. 21).

---

240. Kistemaker, *James*, 410.
241. Kistemaker, *James*, 410.

APPLICATION OF THE TEXT

Often, we think of prayer as primarily a way of asking God for something. Certainly, personal requests and petitions for others are an important part of prayer. But before and beyond that, there is prayer that asks for nothing whatsoever, but simply praises the grandeur and goodness of God. God is worthy of thanksgiving and honor.

In a day and age when the media highlight the glamour of celebrities and the terrors and horrors transpiring in the world, worship by praise seems absurd.[242] When we worship, it does not look like we are *doing* very much—and *we* aren't. Instead, we are looking at what *God* is doing and orienting our behavior toward these realities. Worship is giving attention to the being and acts of God.

Jude's doxology was public and participatory. Through public worship one declares one's allegiance, one's loyalty. Through public worship, the church confesses its allegiance to God above all people, institutions, or value systems that may lay claim upon us. It is verbal witness and testimony that drowns out the hymns and songs of the world that proclaim anti-Christian values. The reason that public versus private worship, corporate rather than individual, is crucial is because worship is a statement to those in earshot that the church will bow to no other gods, but to God alone.

The theme of divine keeping (vv. 1, 13, 21) underscores God's continued presence in the life of the community and throughout the life of each faithful follower of Christ. The goal of this type of language strengthens our hope and outlook about the present and future. Experiencing hope gives us encouragement and helps us to wait patiently and confidently for when we will stand eternally in the divine presence. The promise to stand in the divine presence is hard to imagine or even unimaginable yet Jesus said, "Blessed are the pure in heart for they will see God" (Matt 5:8). Not only will we be in his presence and live,[243] but we likely will wonder if

---

242. Peterson, *Reversed Thunder*, 141.
243. Cf. Gen 16:13; 32:30; Exod 33:18–20; Judg 6:22–23; 13:22.

we ever lived before we were in his presence.[244] To see God will be our greatest joy.

244. Alcorn, *Heaven*, 166.

Bibliography

Alcorn, Randy. *Heaven*. Wheaton, IL: Tyndale House Publishers, 2004.
Aldrete, Gregory S. *Gestures and Acclamations in Ancient Rome*. Baltimore: John Hopkins University Press, 1999.
Alexander, Philip S. "From Son of Adam to Second God: Transformation of the Biblical Enoch." In *Biblical Figures Outside the Bible*, edited by Michael E. Stone and Theodore A. Bergren, 87–122. Harrisburg, PA: Trinity Press International, 1998.
Alter, Robert. *The World of Biblical Literature*. Ann Arbor, MI: Basic Books, 1992.
Anderson, R. Dean, Jr. *Glossary of Greek Rhetorical Terms: Connected to Methods of Argumentation, Figures, and Tropes from Anaximenes to Quintilian*. Contributions to Biblical Exegesis and Theology 24. Leuven: Peeters, 2000.
Aristotle, Longinus, Demetrius. *Poetics. Longinus: On the Sublime. Demetrius: On Style*. Translated by Stephen Halliwell et al. Revised by Donald A. Russell. Loeb Classical Library 199. Cambridge: Harvard University Press, 1995.
Arnott, Peter D. *Public and Performance in the Greek Theatre*. New York: Routledge, 1991.
Arthurs, Jeffrey D. *Preaching as Reminding: Stirring Memory in an Age of Forgetfulness*. Downers Grove, IL: InterVarsity, 2017. Kindle.
Ash, Christopher. *Listen Up! A Practical Guide to Listening to Sermons*. Charlotte, NC: The Good Book Company, 2009.
Ashbrook, James B. "Judgment and Pastoral Counseling." *The Journal of Pastoral Care* 20, no. 1 (1966) 1–9.
Bailey, Nicholas Andrew. "Thetic Constructions in Koine Greek." PhD diss., Vrije Universiteit Amsterdam, 2009.
Baker, William R. *Personal Speech-ethics in the Epistle of James*. Wissenschaftliche Untersuchungen zum Neuen Testament 2/68. Tübingen: Mohr Siebeck, 1995.

Bibliography

Bakker, Egbert J. "Activation and Preservation: The Interdependence of Text and Performance in an Oral Tradition." *Oral Tradition* 8, no. 1 (1993) 5–20.

Barclay, William. *The Letters of John and Jude*. 3rd ed. The New Daily Study Bible. Louisville, KY: Westminster John Knox, 2002.

Bateman, Herbert W., IV. *Jude: Evangelical Exegetical Commentary*. Evangelical Exegetical Commentary. Bellingham, WA: Lexham, 2015.

———. "Rebellion and God's Judgment in the Book of Jude." *Bibliotheca Sacra* 170 (2013) 453–77.

Battezzato, Luigi. "Techniques of Reading and Textual Layout in Ancient Greek Texts." *The Cambridge Classical Journal* 55 (2009) 1–23.

Bauckham, Richard J. *2 Peter, Jude*. Word Biblical Commentary. Vol. 50. Dallas: Word, Incorporated, 1983.

———. *Jude and the Relatives of Jesus in the Early Church*. London: T&T Clark, 2004.

———. "Jude's Exegesis." In *The Catholic Epistles: Critical Readings*, edited by Darian Lockett, 415–70. T&T Clark Critical Readings in Biblical Studies. New York: Bloomsbury, 2021. Kindle.

Bauer, W., F. W. Danker, W. F. Arndt, and F. W. Gingrich. *Greek-English Lexicon of the New Testament and Other Early Christian Literature*. 3rd ed. Chicago: University of Chicago Press, 1999.

Betz, Hans Dieter. "The Problem of Apocalyptic Genre in Greek and Hellenistic Literature: The Case of the Oracle of Trophonius." In *Apocalypticism in the Mediterranean World and the Near East. Proceedings of the International Colloquium on Apocalypticism, Uppsala, August 12–17, 1979*, edited by David Hellholm, 184–208. Tübingen: Mohr, 1983.

Bigg, Charles. *A Critical and Exegetical Commentary on the Epistles of St. Peter and St. Jude*. International Critical Commentary on the Holy Scriptures of the Old and New Testaments 42. New York: Charles Scribner's Sons, 1901.

Blum, Edwin A. "Jude." In *The Expositor's Bible Commentary*. Vol. 13. Pradis CD-ROM Book Version: 4.0.2, edited by Frank E. Gaebelein, n.p. Grand Rapids: Zondervan, 1995.

Blumell, Lincoln H. "The Message and the Medium: Some Observations on Epistolary Communication in Late Antiquity." *Journal of Greco-Roman Christianity and Judaism* 10 (2014) 24–67.

Boegehold, Alan L. *When a Gesture Was Expected: A Selection of Examples from Archaic and Classical Greek Literature*. Princeton: Princeton University, 1999.

Brannan, Rick. *Apostolic Fathers Greek-English Interlinear*. Bellingham, WA: Lexham, 2011.

Briggs, Richard S. "Speech-Act Theory." In *Words and the Word: Explorations in Biblical Interpretation & Literary Theory*, edited by David G. Firth and Jamie A. Grant, 75–110. Downers Grove, IL: InterVarsity, 2008.

Brosend, William. "The Letter of Jude: A Rhetoric of Excess or an Excess of Rhetoric?" *Interpretation* 60 (2006) 292–305.

Bibliography

Brown, Francis, Samuel Rolles Driver, and Charles Augustus Briggs. *Enhanced Brown-Driver-Briggs Hebrew and English Lexicon*. Oxford: Clarendon, 1977.

Cambron-Goulet, Mathilde. "Orality in Philosophical Epistles." In *Between Orality and Literacy: Communication and Adaptation in Antiquity*, edited by Ruth Scodel, 148–74. Orality and Literacy in the Ancient World 10. Mnemosyne Supplements 367. Leiden: Brill, 2014.

Cassius, Dio. *Roman History, Volume I: Books 1–11*. Translated by Earnest Cary and Herbert B. Foster. Loeb Classical Library 32. Cambridge: Harvard University Press, 1914.

Chaniotis, Angelos. "Listening to Stones: Orality and Emotions in Ancient Inscriptions." In *Epigraphy and Historical Sciences*, edited by J. Davies and J. Wilkes, 299–328. Oxford: Oxford University, 2012.

Charles, J. Daryl. "Literary Artifice in the Epistle of Jude." *Zeitschrift Für Die Neutestamentliche Wissenschaft Und Die Kunde Der Älteren Kirche* 82, no. 1–2 (1991) 122–23.

———. "Polemic and Persuasion: Typological and Rhetorical Perspectives on the Letter of Jude." In *The Catholic Epistles: Critical Readings*, edited by Darian R. Lockett, 892–936. New York: Bloomsbury, 2021.

Charles, Robert Henry, ed. "The Assumption of Moses." In *Pseudepigrapha of the Old Testament*. Vol. 2. Oxford: Clarendon, 1913.

Cicero. *Letters to Atticus, Volume I*. Edited and translated by D. R. Shackleton Bailey. Loeb Classical Library 7. Cambridge: Harvard University Press, 1999.

———. *Letters to Quintus and Brutus. Letter Fragments. Letter to Octavian. Invectives. Handbook of Electioneering*. Edited and translated by D. R. Shackleton Bailey. Loeb Classical Library 462. Cambridge: Harvard University Press, 2002.

———. *On the Orator: Book 3. On Fate. Stoic Paradoxes. Divisions of Oratory*. Translated by H. Rackham. Loeb Classical Library 349. Cambridge: Harvard University Press, 1942.

———. *Pro Caelio. De Provinciis Consularibus. Pro Balbo*. Translated by R. Gardner. Loeb Classical Library 447. Cambridge: Harvard University Press, 1958.

Clark, Herbert H., and Richard J. Gerrig. "Quotations as Demonstrations." *Language* 66, no. 4 (1990) 764–805.

Cosby, Michael R. *The Rhetorical Composition and Function of Hebrews 11: In Light of Example Lists in Antiquity*. Macon: Mercer University Press, 1988.

Crawford, Albert. Unpublished "Notes for Systematic Theology I." Grand Rapids Baptist Seminary, Fall 1999.

Davids, Peter H. *The Letters of 2 Peter and Jude*. The Pillar New Testament Commentary. Grand Rapids: Eerdmans, 2006.

De Feo, Stefano. "A Critical Analysis of the Use of the Verb ἀναγινώσκω in the *Corpus Paulinum*: A Reappraisal of the Reading Practice in Early Christianity." *Annali di scienze religiose* 13 (2020) 297–335.

Bibliography

Devine, A. M., and Laurence D. Stephens. *The Prosody of Greek Speech*. New York: Oxford University Press, 1994.

De Waal, Kayle B. *An Aural Performance Analysis of Revelation 1 and 11*. Studies in Biblical Literature 163. New York: Peter Lang, 2015.

Dinkler, Michal Beth. *Silent Statements: Narrative Representations of Speech and Silence in the Gospel of Luke*. Beihefte zur Zeitschrift für die neutestamentliche Wissenschaft 191. Berlin: De Gruyter, 2013.

Dionysius of Halicarnassus. *Critical Essays, Volume II: On Literary Composition. Dinarchus. Letters to Ammaeus and Pompeius*. Translated by Stephen Usher. Loeb Classical Library 466. Cambridge: Harvard University Press, 1985.

Dobbs-Allsopp, F. W. *On Biblical Poetry*. New York: Oxford University Press, 2015. Kindle.

Dodson, J. R. *The "Powers" of Personification: Rhetorical Purpose in the "Book of Wisdom" and the Letter to the Romans*. Beihefte zur Zeitschrift fur die neutestamentliche Wissenschaft 161. Berlin: De Gruyter, 2008.

Donelson, Lewis R. *I and II Peter, and Jude: A Commentary*. New Testament Library. Louisville, KY: Westminster, 2010.

Du Toit, Andrie. "Vilification as a Pragmatic Device in Early Christian Epistolography." In *Focusing on Paul: Persuasion and Theological Design in Romans and Galatians*, edited by Cilliers Breytenbach and David S. du Toit, 45–56. Beihefte zur Zeitschrift fur die neutestamentliche Wissenschaft 151. Berlin: Walter de Gruyter, 2012.

Eusebius. *Ecclesiastical History, Volume I: Books 1–5*. Translated by Kirsopp Lake. Loeb Classical Library 153. Cambridge: Harvard University Press, 1926.

Fögen, Thorsten. "Ancient Approaches to Letter Writing and the Configuration of Communities through Epistles." In *Letters and Communities, Studies in the Socio-Political Dimensions of Ancient Epistolography*, edited by Paola Ceccarelli et al., 46–82. Oxford: Oxford University Press, 2018.

Foley, John B. "An Aural Basis for Oral Liturgical Prayer." *Worship* 56, no. 2 (1982) 132–52.

Foley, John Miles. "Memory in Oral Tradition." In *Performing the Gospel: Orality, Memory, and Mark*, edited by Richard A. Horsley et al., 83–96. Minneapolis: Fortress, 2011.

Franke, William. "At the Creative Source of the Arts: Poetry as Prophecy in a Negative Theological Key." *Prophetic Witness and the Reimagining of the World: Poetry, Theology and Philosophy in Dialogue—Power of the World V*, edited by Mark S. Burrows, Hilary Davies, and Josephine von Zitzewitz, n.p. Routledge Studies in Religion. New York: Routledge, 2021.

French, Patrice L. "Toward an Explanation of Phonetic Symbolism." *Word* 28:3 (1977) 305–22.

Geller, Stephen A. "Were the Prophets Poets?" *Proof* 3, no. 2 (1983) 211–21.

"Gemara." In *Baker Encyclopedia of the Bible*, edited by Walter A. Elwell and Barry J. Beitzel, 844. Grand Rapids: Baker Book House, 1988.

Bibliography

Green, E. Michael. *2 Peter and Jude*. Downers Grove, IL: InterVarsity, 2009.

Gunther, John J. "The Alexandrian Epistle of Jude." *New Testament Studies* 30 (1984) 549–62.

Haidt, Jonathan. *The Righteous Mind: Why Good People Are Divided by Politics and Religion*. New York: Pantheon, 2012.

Harris, William V. *Ancient Literacy*. Cambridge: Harvard University Press, 1989.

Harvey, John D. *Listening to the Text: Oral Patterning in Paul's Letters*. ETS Studies. Grand Rapids, Baker Books, 1998.

Hearon, Holly E. "Characters in Text and Performance: The Gospel of John." In *From Text to Performance: Narrative and Performance Criticisms in Dialogue and Debate*, edited by Kelly R. Iverson, 53–79. Biblical Performance Criticism 10. Eugene, OR: Cascade, 2014.

Heath, John. *The Talking Greeks: Speech, Animals, and the Other in Homer, Aeschylus, and Plato*. New York: Cambridge University Press, 2005.

Heffelfinger, Katie M. "More than Mere Ornamentation." *PIBA* 36 (2013) 36–54.

Heilmann, Jan. "Reading Early New Testament Manuscripts." In *Material Aspects of Reading in Ancient and Medieval Cultures: Materiality, Presence and Performance*, edited by Anna Krauß, Jonas Leipziger, and Friederike Schücking-Jungblut, 177–96. Schriftenreihe des Sonderforschungsbereichs 933. Band 26. Berlin: De Gruyter, 2020.

Hezser, Catherine. *Jewish Literacy in Roman Palestine*. Texts and Studies in Ancient Judaism 81. Tübingen: Mohr Siebeck, 2001.

Hibbitts, Bernard J. "'Coming to Our Senses': Communication and Legal Expression in Performance Cultures." *Emory Law Journal* 41, no. 4 (1992) 874–960.

Holland, Glenn S. "'Frightening You with Letters': Traces of Performance in the Letters of Paul." *Proceedings of the Eastern Great Lakes and Midwest Biblical Societies* 26 (2006) 1–21.

Hollander, Harm W. "The Attitude towards Christians Who Are Doubting: Jude 22–3 and the Text of Zechariah 3." In *The Book of Zechariah and Its Influence*, edited by Christopher Tuckett, 123–34. Routledge Revivals. Reprint. New York: Routledge, 2018. Kindle.

Homer. *Odyssey, Volume I: Books 1–12*. Translated by A. T. Murray. Revised by George E. Dimock. Loeb Classical Library 104. Cambridge: Harvard University Press, 1919.

Hultin, Jeremy F. "The Literary Relationships Among 1 Peter, 2 Peter, and Jude. In *Reading 1–2 Peter and Jude: A Resource for Students*, edited by Troy W. Martin and Eric Farrel Mason, 27–45. Atlanta: Society of Biblical Literature, 2014.

Isocrates. *To Demonicus. To Nicocles. Nicocles or the Cyprians. Panegyricus. To Philip. Archidamus.* Translated by George Norlin. Loeb Classical Library 209. Cambridge: Harvard University Press, 1928.

Bibliography

Iverson, Kelly R. "A Centurion's 'Confession': A Performance-Critical Analysis of Mark 15:39." *Journal of Biblical Literature* 130 (2011) 329–50.

Jakobson, Roman, and Linda R. Waugh. *The Sound Shape of Language*. Berlin: De Gruyter, 2002.

Janzen, Waldemar. *Mourning Cry and Woe Oracle*. Beihefte zur Zeitschrift für die alttestamentliche Wissenschaft 125. Berlin: De Gruyter, 1972.

Jeal, Roy. *Integrating Theology and Ethics in Ephesians: The Ethos of Communication*. Studies in the Bible and Early Christianity 43. Lewiston, NY: E. Mellen, 2000.

Johnson, William A. *Readers and Reading Culture in the High Roman Empire: A Study of Elite Communities*. New York: Oxford University Press, 2010.

Josephus, Flavius, and William Whiston. *The Works of Josephus: Complete and Unabridged*. Peabody, MA: Hendrickson, 1987.

Joubert, Stephen J. "Facing the Past: Transtextual Relationships and Historical Understanding in the Letter of Jude." *Biblische Zeitschrift* 42, no. 1 (September 1998) 56–70.

———. "Language, Ideology and the Social Context of the Letter of Jude." *Neotestamentica* 24, no. 2 (1990) 335–49.

———. "Persuasion in the Letter of Jude." *Journal for the Study of the New Testament* 58 (1995) 75–87.

Kelly, J. N. D. *The Epistles of Peter and of Jude*. Black's New Testament Commentary. London: Continuum, 1969.

Keltner, Dacher, and Jonathan Haidt. "Approaching Awe, a Moral, Spiritual, and Aesthetic Emotion." *Cognition and Emotion* 17, no. 2 (2003) 297–314.

Kent, Grenville J. R. *Say It Again, Sam: A Literary and Filmic Study of Narrative Repetition in 1 Samuel 28*. Eugene, OR: Pickwick, 2011.

Kistemaker, Simon J. *James, Epistles of John, Peter, and Jude*. Grand Rapids: Baker, 1996.

Klauck, Hans-Josef, and Daniel P. Bailey. *Ancient Letters and the New Testament: A Guide to Context and Exegesis*. Waco: Baylor University Press, 2006.

Knight, Jonathan. *2 Peter and Jude*. Sheffield, England: Sheffield Academic, 1995.

Kraftchick, Steven J. *Jude & 2 Peter*. Abingdon New Testament Commentaries. Nashville: Abingdon, 2002.

Laird, Benjamin. "Muratorian Fragment." In *The Lexham Bible Dictionary*, edited by John D. Barry et al. Bellingham, WA: Lexham, 2016.

Lateiner, Donald. *Sardonic Smile: Nonverbal Behavior in Homeric Epic*. Ann Arbor: University of Michigan Press, 1998.

Leach, John. *Responding to Preaching*. Cambridge: Grove, 1997.

Lee, Margaret, and Bernard Scott. *Sound Mapping in the New Testament*. Salem, OR: Polebridge, 2009.

Lewis, Gordon R., and Bruce A. Demarest. *Integrative Theology: Three Volumes in One*. Grand Rapids: Zondervan, 1996.

Lincoln, Andrew T. *Ephesians*. Vol. 42. Word Biblical Commentary. Grand Rapids: Zondervan, 1990.

Bibliography

Lockett, Darian R. "Objects of Mercy in Jude: The Prophetic Background of Jude 22–23." *The Catholic Biblical Quarterly* 77, no. 2 (2015) 322–36.

Loubser, J. A. "Invoking the Ancestors: Some Socio-Rhetorical Aspects of the Genealogies in the Gospels of Matthew and Luke." *Neotestamenica* 39, no. 1 (2005) 127–40.

Lucian. *How to Write History. The Dipsads. Saturnalia. Herodotus or Aetion. Zeuxis or Antiochus. A Slip of the Tongue in Greeting. Apology for the "Salaried Posts in Great Houses." Harmonides. A Conversation with Hesiod. The Scythian or The Consul. Hermotimus or Concerning the Sects. To One Who Said "You're a Prometheus in Words." The Ship or The Wishes.* Translated by K. Kilburn. Loeb Classical Library 430. Cambridge: Harvard University Press, 1959.

Mangina, Joseph L. *Karl Barth: Theologian of Christian Witness*. Burlington, VT: Ashgate, 2004.

Martin, Richard P. "Similes and Performance." In *Written Voices, Spoken Signs: Tradition, Performance, and the Epic Text*, edited by Egbert J. Bakker and Ahuvia Kahane, 138–66. Cambridge: Harvard University Press, 1997.

Mathews, Kenneth A. *Genesis 1–11:26*. Vol. 1A. The New American Commentary. Nashville: Broadman & Holman, 1996.

Mayor, J. B. "The General Epistle of Jude." In vol. 5 of *The Expositor's Greek Testament*, edited by W. Robertson Nicoll, 209–77. New York: George H. Doran, n.d.

McConachie, Bruce. *Engaging Audiences: A Cognitive Approach to Spectating in the Theatre*. New York: Palgrave Macmillan, 2008.

Mcneill, David, et al. "Abstract Deixis." *Semiotica* 95–1/2 (July 1993) 5–19.

Michaels, J. Ramsey. "Finding Yourself an Intercessor: New Testament Prayer from Hebrews to Jude." In *Into God's Presence: Prayer in the New Testament*, edited by Richard N. Longenecker 228–51. Grand Rapids: Eerdmans, 2002.

Miller, Marvin Lloyd. *Performances of Ancient Jewish Letters: From Elephantine to MMT*. Journal of Ancient Judaism. Supplements 20. Bristol, CT: Vandenhoeck & Ruprecht, 2015.

Minchin, Elizabeth. "Similes in Homer, Image, Mind's Eye, and Memory." In *Speaking Volumes: Orality and Literacy in the Greek and Roman World*, edited by Janet Watson, 25–52. Mnemosyne, Supplements 218. Leiden: Brill, 2017.

Moo, Douglass J. *2 Peter, Jude*. NIV Application Commentary. Grand Rapids, Zondervan, 1996.

Murray, Penelope. "Poetic Inspiration." In *A Companion to Ancient Aesthetics*, edited by Pierre Destrée and Penelope Murray, 158–75. Chichester: Wiley & Sons, 2015.

Nässelqvist, Dan. *Public Reading in Early Christianity: Lectors, Manuscripts, and Sound in the Oral Delivery of John 1–4*. Supplements to Novum Testamentum 163. Leiden: Brill, 2016.

NET Bible, Full Notes Edition. Nashville: Thomas Nelson, 2019.

Bibliography

Neyrey, Jerome H. *2 Peter, Jude: A New Translation with Introduction and Commentary.* Vol. 37C. Anchor Yale Bible. New Haven: Yale University Press, 2008.

Nickelsburg, George W. E. *1 Enoch 1: A Commentary on the Book of 1 Enoch.* Hermeneia. Minneapolis: Fortress, 2001.

Niditch, Susan. *Oral World and Written Word.* Library of Ancient Israel. Edited by Douglas A. Knight. Louisville, KY: Westminster, 1996.

Novella, Steven. *Your Deceptive Mind: A Scientific Guide to Critical Thinking Skills.* Chantilly, VA: Teaching Company, 2012.

Nünlist, Rene. *The Ancient Critic at Work: Terms and Concepts of Literary Criticism in Greek Scholia.* Cambridge: Cambridge University Press, 2009.

Oestreich, Bernhard. *Performance Criticism in the Pauline Letters.* Translated by Lindsay Elias and Brent Blum. Biblical Performance Criticism 14. Eugene, OR: Cascade, 2016.

O'Leary, Stephen D. "Apocalyptic Argument and the Anticipation of Catastrophe: The Prediction of Risk and the Risks of Prediction." *Argumentation* 11 (1997) 293–313.

———. "A Dramatistic Theory of Apocalyptic Rhetoric." *Quarterly Journal of Speech* 79, no. 4 (1993) 385–426.

Olrik, Axel. *Principles for Oral Narrative Research.* Bloomington: Indiana University Press, 1992.

Painter, John, and David A. deSilva. *James and Jude.* Paideia: Commentaries on the New Testament. Grand Rapids: Baker, 2012.

Perkins, Pheme. *First and Second Peter, James, and Jude.* Interpretation: A Bible Commentary for Teaching and Preaching. Louisville: John Knox, 2012.

Perry, Peter S. *Insights from Performance Criticism. Reading the Bible in the 21st Century: Insights.* Minneapolis: Fortress, 2016.

Peterson, Eugene H. *Reversed Thunder: The Revelation of John and the Praying Imagination.* San Francisco: HarperSanFrancisco, 1991.

Petronius, Seneca. *Satyricon. Apocolocyntosis.* Edited and translated by Gareth Schmeling. Loeb Classical Library 15. Cambridge: Harvard University Press, 2020.

Plato. *Euthyphro. Apology. Crito. Phaedo.* Translated by E. Jones and W. Preddy. Loeb Classical Library 36. Cambridge: Harvard University Press, 2017.

———. *Lysis. Symposium. Gorgias.* Translated by W. R. M. Lamb. Loeb Classical Library 166. Cambridge: Harvard University Press, 1925.

———. *Statesman. Philebus. Ion.* Translated by H. N. Fowler and W. R. M. Lamb. Loeb Classical Library 164. Cambridge: Harvard University Press, 1925.

Plautus. *Amphitryon. The Comedy of Asses. The Pot of Gold. The Two Bacchises. The Captives.* Edited and translated by Wolfgang de Melo. Loeb Classical Library 60. Cambridge: Harvard University Press, 2011.

Pliny the Younger. *Letters, Volume I: Books 1–7.* Translated by Betty Radice. Loeb Classical Library 55. Cambridge: Harvard University Press, 1969.

Bibliography

Plutarch. *Lives, Volume III: Pericles and Fabius Maximus. Nicias and Crassus.* Translated by Bernadotte Perrin. Loeb Classical Library 65. Cambridge: Harvard University Press, 1916.

Porter, Stanley E. *Handbook of Classical Rhetoric in the Hellenistic Period, 330 B.C–A.D. 400.* New York: SBL, 1997.

Porter, Stanley E., and Andrew W. Pitts. *Fundamentals of New Testament Textual Criticism.* Grand Rapids: Eerdmans, 2015.

Pulleyn, Simon. *Prayer in Greek Religion.* Oxford: Clarendon, 1997.

Reece, Steve. *Paul's Large Letters: Paul's Autographic Subscriptions in the Light of Ancient Epistolary Conventions.* The Library of New Testament Studies 561. New York: Bloomsbury, 2017.

Reese, Ruth Anne. *2 Peter and Jude.* Two Horizons New Testament Commentary. Grand Rapids: Eerdmans, 2007. Kindle.

Reicke, Bo. *The Epistles of James, Peter, and Jude.* 2nd ed. Anchor Bible Vol. 37. Garden City, NY: Doubleday, 1964.

Richards, E. Randolph. *Paul and First-Century Letter Writing: Secretaries, Composition and Collection.* Downers Grove, IL, InterVarsity, 2004.

Robinson, Alexandra. *Jude on the Attack: A Comparative Analysis of the Epistle of Jude, Jewish Judgement Oracles, and Greco-Roman Invective.* New York: Bloomsbury, 2018.

Roudkovski, Viktor. "James, Brother of Jesus." In *The Lexham Bible Dictionary*, edited by John D. Barry et al., n.p. Bellingham, WA: Lexham, 2016.

Ryken, Leland. *Words of Delight: A Literary Introduction to the Bible.* 2nd edition. Grand Rapids: Baker Book House, 1992.

Sacks, Oliver. *Musicophilia: Tales of Music and the Brain.* New York: Alfred A. Knopf, 2008.

Saenger, Paul. *Space Between Words: The Origins of Silent Reading.* Stanford: Stanford University Press, 1997.

Schart, Aaron. "Deathly Silence and Apocalyptic Noise: Observations on the Soundscape of the Book of the Twelve." *Verbum et Ecclesia* 31, no. 1 (July 2010) 1–5.

Schreiner, Thomas R. *1, 2 Peter, Jude.* The New American Commentary 37. Nashville: Broadman & Holman, 2003.

Seal, David. "Jude Delivered." *Biblica* 99, no. 1 (2018) 93–108.

———. "A Performance Critical Analysis of the Lukan Parable." *Review and Expositor* 115, no. 2 (2018) 243–53.

Seal, David, and Michael Partridge. *Performing Scripture.* Cambridge: Grove, 2019.

Seneca. *Epistles 1–65.* Translated by Richard M. Gummere. Loeb Classical Library 75. Cambridge: Harvard University Press, 1917.

———. *Epistles 66–92.* Translated by Richard M Gummere. Loeb Classical Library 76. Cambridge: Harvard University Press, 1920.

Seneca the Elder. *Declamations, Volume I: Controversiae, Books 1–6.* Translated by Michael Winterbottom. Loeb Classical Library 463. Cambridge: Harvard University Press, 1974.

Bibliography

Serafim, Andreas. *Attic Oratory and Performance*. Routledge Monographs in Classical Studies. New York: Taylor and Francis, 2017. Kindle.

Shiell, William David. *Delivery from Memory: The Effect of Performance on Early Christian Audience*. Eugene, OR: Cascade, 2011.

———. *Reading Acts: The Lector and the Early Christian Audience*. Boston: Brill, 2004.

Shiner, Whitney. "Oral Performance of the New Testament." In *The Bible in Ancient and Modern Media: Story and Performance*, edited by Holy E. Hearon and Philip Ruge-Jones, 49–63. Biblical Performance Criticism 1. Eugene, OR: Cascade, 2009.

———. *Proclaiming the Gospel: First-Century Performance of Mark*. Harrisburg, PA: Trinity Press International, 2003.

Shrum, L. J., and Tina M. Lowrey. "Sounds Convey Meaning: The Implications of Phonetic Symbolism for Band Name Construction." In *Psycholinguistic Phenomena in Marketing Communications*, edited by Tina M. Lowery, 39–58. Mahwah, NJ: Erlbaum, 2007.

Skeat, T. C. "Was Papyrus Regarded as 'Cheap' or 'Expensive' in the Ancient World?" *Aegyptus* 75 (1995) 74–93.

Snyder, H. Gregory. *Teachers and Texts in the Ancient World*. Religion in the First Christian Centuries. New York: Routledge, 2000. Kindle.

Sproul, R. C. *How Should I Live in This World?* Vol. 5. The Crucial Questions Series. Lake Mary, FL: Reformation Trust Publishing, 2009.

Stanford, William Bedell. *Greek Tragedy and the Emotions: An Introductory Study*. London: Routledge & Kegan Paul, 1983.

———. *The Sound of Greek: Studies in the Greek Theory and Practice of Euphony*. Berkeley: University of California Press, 1967.

Stanley, Christopher D. "Paul and Homer: Greco-Roman Citation Practice in the First Century." *Novum Testamentum* 32, no. 1 (1990) 48–78.

Stirewalt, M. Luther, Jr. *Paul, the Letter Writer*. Grand Rapids: Eerdmans, 2003.

Suetonius. *Lives of the Caesars, Volume II: Claudius. Nero. Galba, Otho, and Vitellius. Vespasian. Titus, Domitian. Lives of Illustrious Men: Grammarians and Rhetoricians. Poets (Terence. Virgil. Horace. Tibullus. Persius. Lucan). Lives of Pliny the Elder and Passienus Crispus*. Translated by J. C. Rolfe. Loeb Classical Library 38. Cambridge: Harvard University Press, 1914.

Thurén, Lauri. "Hey Jude! Asking for the Original Situation and Message of a Catholic Epistle." *New Testament Studies* 43 (1997) 451–65.

Tiles, Jim E. *Moral Measures: An Introduction to Ethics West and East*. New York: Routledge, 2000.

Upton, Bridget Gilfillan. *Hearing Mark's Endings: Listening to Ancient Popular Texts through Speech Act Theory*. Biblical Interpretation Series 79. Boston: Brill, 2006.

Valiavitcharska, Vessela. *Rhetoric and Rhythm in Byzantium: The Sound of Persuasion*. New York: Cambridge University Press, 2013.

Vearncombe, Erin K. "Codex." In *The Dictionary of the Bible and Ancient Media*, edited by Tom Thatcher et al., 52–53. London: Bloomsbury, 2017.

Bibliography

Wallaschek, Richard. *Primitive Music: An Inquiry into the Origin and Development of Music, Songs, Instruments, Dances, and Pantomimes of Savage Races, with Musical Examples.* London: Longmans, Green, and Co. 1893.

Ward, Richard F., and David J. Trobisch. *Bringing the Word to Life: Engaging the New Testament through Performing It.* Grand Rapids: Eerdmans, 2013.

Watson, Duane Frederick. "The Epistolary Rhetoric of 1 Peter, 2 Peter, and Jude." In *Reading 1–2 Peter and Jude: A Resource for Students*, edited by Eric F. Mason & Troy W. Martin, 47–62. Atlanta: Society of Biblical Literature, 2014.

———. *Invention, Arrangement, and Style. Rhetorical Criticism of Jude and 2 Peter.* Atlanta: Society of Biblical Literature, 1988.

———. "Jude." In *The New Interpreter's Bible Commentary. Ephesians, Philippians, Colossians, 1 & 2 Thessalonians, 1 & 2 Timothy, Titus, Philemon, Hebrews, James, 1 & 2 Peter, 1, 2 & 3 John, Jude, Revelation.* Vol. 10, edited by J. Paul Sampley, 473–500. Nashville: Abingdon, 2015.

Webb, Robert L. "The Use of 'Story' in the Letter of Jude: Rhetorical Strategies of Jude's Narrative Episodes." *Journal for the Study of the New Testament* 31, no. 1 (September 2008) 53–87.

Weima, Jeffrey A. D. *Neglected Endings: The Significance of the Pauline Letter Closings.* Sheffield, England: Sheffield Academic, 1994.

Wheaton, David H. "Jude." In *The New Bible Commentary*, edited by Donald Guthrie et al., 1274–78. Reprint. Grand Rapids: Eerdmans, 1991.

Whitenton, Michael. "Feeling the Silence: A Moment-by-Moment Account of Emotions at the End of Mark (16:1–8)." *Catholic Biblical Quarterly* 78 (2016) 272–89.

Wierenga, Micah. "Church Fathers." In *The Lexham Bible Dictionary*, edited by John D. Barry et al., n.p. Bellingham, WA: Lexham, 2016.

Wierzbicka, Anna. "The Semantics of Direct and Indirect Discourse." *Papers in Linguistics* 1 (1974) 267–307.

Williams, Catrin H. "How Scripture 'Speaks': Insights from the Study of Ancient Media Culture." In *Methodology in the Use of the Old Testament in the New: Context and Criteria*, edited by David Allen and Steve Smith, 53–69. Library of New Testament Studies 579. London: Bloomsbury, 2019.

Winsbury, Rex. *The Roman Book: Books, Publishing and Performance in Classical Rome.* Classical Literature and Society. London: Bloomsbury, 2009.

Wise, Michael O., Martin G. Abegg Jr., and Edward M. Cook. *The Dead Sea Scrolls: A New Translation.* New York: HarperOne, 2005.

Witherington, Ben, III. *What's in the Word. Rethinking the Socio-Rhetorical Character of the New Testament.* Waco: Baylor University Press, 2009.

Wright, Brian J. *Communal Reading in the Time of Jesus: A Window into Early Christian Reading Practices.* Minneapolis: Fortress, 2017.

www.ingramcontent.com/pod-product-compliance
Lightning Source LLC
Chambersburg PA
CBHW070632220426
R18178600001B/R181786PG43193CBX00014B/17